Lucille Milani is Clothing Instructor,
Merced College and former Home Advisor,
University of California Agricultural
Extension Service, Madera County.

Tailoring
The Easy Way

LUCILLE MILANI

A SPECTRUM BOOK

Prentice-Hall, Inc., Englewood Cliffs, New Jersey

Library of Congress Cataloging in Publication Data

Milani, Lucille.
  Tailoring the easy way.

  (The Creative handcrafts series) (A Spectrum
Book)
  Includes index.
  1. tailoring. 2. tailoring (women's) I. title.
TT580.M45   646.4   76-3691
ISBN 0-13-882183-6
ISBN 0-13-882175-5 pbk.

© 1976 by Prentice-Hall, Inc., Englewood Cliffs, New Jersey

A Spectrum Book

10 9 8 7 6 5 4 3 2 1

Printed in the United States of America

Prentice-Hall International, Inc., *London*
Prentice-Hall of Australia Pty. Limited, *Sydney*
Prentice-Hall of Canada, Ltd., *Toronto*
Prentice-Hall of India Private Limited, *New Delhi*
Prentice-Hall of Japan, Inc., *Tokyo*
Prentice-Hall of Southeast Asia Pte. Ltd., *Singapore*

Contents

2

WOMEN'S COATS AND SUITS   13

3

MEN'S JACKETS AND PANTS   77

Preface

I became interested in writing a tailoring manual which included both men's and women's garments mostly out of need in my own tailoring classes. I had difficulty finding a text that students could use as a reference and as a supplement to my class lectures.

Most pattern company instructions enable you to *sew* a coat or jacket, but in order to end with a professional-looking *tailored* garment, certain other steps must be followed during construction.

Techniques for tailoring men's and women's garments are so different that they are rarely both discussed under the same cover. I wanted this information at my fingertips and felt a need for students to have easy access to it also. I've always felt that techniques need not be memorized so long as one can easily find the information when needed. This text is intended to serve both as a reference for experienced tailors and as a step-by-step guide for beginners.

My main goal has always been to help students *enjoy* tailoring so they will want to continue tailoring once their initial project is completed.

Lucille A. Milani

1
Introduction

FABRIC SELECTION AND PREPARATION

There is really no limit to the type of fabric you can use for your coat or jacket. Some fabrics will be easier to work with than others, and the cost varies a great deal. Fabric choice should depend on your experience, your climate, and your economics.

If you want to use this project strictly as a sample for your first custom-tailoring effort, I would encourage you to buy a moderately priced fabric. However, if you are familiar with tailoring, then perhaps you have enough knowledge and skills to go all out on a fine piece of wool or knit.

One word of caution on using knits—use a good grade of double knit for good results. Do not use a women's dress knit fabric and expect to produce a high-grade tailored jacket. Menswear double knits are firmer and denser and give better results in a man's jacket.

Fine wools are quite easy to tailor. The main thing is that you should use a fabric that *you* like if you are making yourself a coat, or use a fabric that the other person likes if you are sewing for someone else.

The only fabrics I would not recommend for your first attempt would be tightly woven synthetics or tightly woven gabardines. Once you understand the techniques, you can tailor anything you like. You'll quickly find out what fabrics you prefer to work with and how it will react.

For the average home sewer, plaids are not harder to work on once they are properly cut. Avoid patterns with a lot of seams when using a plaid. Don't forget to allow extra yardage when working with large plaids.

Lining for your garment should be of a good grade rayon or silk. Some polyesters are also excellent. A lining should be slick and smooth to enable the wearer to slip in and out of the garment easily. It is usually necessary only to steam press the rayon or silk with your iron to prepare it for sewing. Washable linings may be dampened and then put in the dryer in order to preshrink them.

Whatever you choose, be sure to prepare your fabric for sewing. Knits are stretched when the manufacturer puts them on the bolt, and they need to be put back to their original shape. Woolens must also be preshrunk. Many dry cleaning establishments will preshrink your woolens for a nominal cost. The following rules may help you to decide what treatment, if any, is required:

1. Fabrics such as woolens (flannel types, for instance) having an open, loose weave usually need shrinking.

2. Fabrics labeled with a label indicating a shrinkage treatment gener-

ally do not require further processing unless they need straightening. This may involve "sheet treating" or pressing with a steam iron or having the fabric steamed by a professional.
3. Wool crepes should never be "sheet treated." Press only with the steam iron to straighten or have them steamed professionally.

If your wool fabric needs to be "sheet treated" for shrinking and/or straightening, follow these steps:

1. Ends should be torn or a thread pulled and the ends trimmed.

2. Leave fabric folded as purchased. The right side should be inside.

3. Wet a sheet, and then wring it out to spread the moisture evenly throughout the sheet. There should be no dry or excessively wet spots. Open sheet and spread out on a table. Place the wool folded lengthwise on the center section (See Fig. 1).

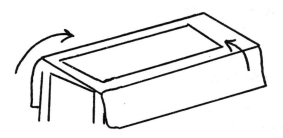

Figure 1

4. Fold the long sides of the sheet over the center section. Fold sheet over and over in deep folds (about 12 inches, 30.5 cm) up to the middle (See Fig. 2). Do the same from the opposite end. Wrap with paper to prevent drying out too quickly and let stand two hours.

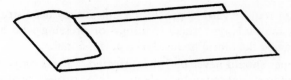

Figure 2

5. Unfold and lay fabric out on a flat surface, straightening grain by "squaring to the table," and smooth with your hands. Allow to dry. Do not hang. It may be necessary to turn the fabric in order to allow it to dry evenly.

6. If pressing is necessary, leave cloth folded and press lightly with the lengthwise grain, using a steam iron. Do not shove the cloth along while pressing.

Washable knits can be preshrunk in the washer and dryer—and do the same with any cottons or muslin used in the jacket or coat. Simply dip tape and pocket material in hot water and hang to dry. It is easiest to fold the card to allow for shrinkage and leave the tape on it to dry.

TAILORING STITCHES

For your reference, here are the descriptions and illustrations of stitching terminology used in tailoring. They are easy enough, but I urge you to take the time and patience to use them correctly.

TAILORING BASTING

Tailoring basting is usually done in a contrasting thread on the right side of the fabric and is eventually removed from the garment.

Insert your needle horizontally, right to left. Take a tiny stitch and drop down, then repeat about two inches directly under the first stitch. You will have long, slanted, vertical stitches. The long stitches show on the right side, the small stitches on the wrong side (See Fig. 3).

Figure 3

PAD-STITCHING

Pad-stitching is done with matching thread on the wrong side of the garment. These stitches stay in and are used to anchor and mold. They are actually miniature tailor-basting stitches. You insert the needle as you do in tailor-basting, but you only take a pinprick, and your next stitch will be only ½ inch down. In this stitch, the pinprick is on the *right* side (See Fig. 4).

Figure 4

RUNNING STITCH

The running stitch is usually done in matching thread. It is actually a small, neat, basting stitch about ¼ inch long used to anchor cotton twill tape (See Fig. 5).

Figure 5

BACKSTITCH

The backstitch looks like a running stitch on the right side and like machine-stitching on the wrong side. It is used to provide strong anchoring.

Insert your needle under the fabric twice the length of the desired finished stitch. After you bring up your needle, insert it between the upraised thread and the last stitch on top, again making the underneath stitch twice the length of the top stitch. Continue in this manner (See Fig. 6).

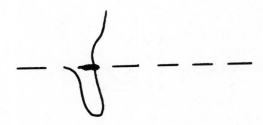

Figure 6

FELLING STITCH

The felling stitch is a tiny vertical stitch that is sometimes called a hem stitch. It is used in the collar and other areas requiring precision sewing. Insert the needle on the right side and sew horizontally. Take a tiny bite of each piece of fabric, as illustrated in Figure 7. Each stitch is sewn quite close to each preceding stitch.

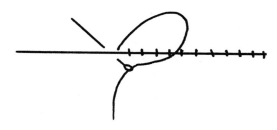

Figure 7

CATCH-STITCH

The catch-stitch is a very important stitch used to catch one seam to another without any stitches showing on the right side. It is also used to anchor pads to interfacing in men's jackets and to secure hems to the interfacing in some tailored garments. It is done in matching thread and is always worked left to right (unless you're left handed).

Insert your needle in the fabric from the right. Take a tiny stitch. Continue working horizontally. These stitches may be as large or small as you wish, depending on what you are sewing together (See Fig. 8).

Figure 8

STAB-STITCH

The stab-stitch is used to hold the shoulder pads in place. Because of the thickness of the materials being handled, only one stitch can be taken at a time. Push the needle directly through all thicknesses to the other side. Make each stitch securely, but don't pull the stitches too tight (See Fig. 9).

Figure 9

SLIPSTITCH

The slipstitch is used for a turned edge or where it's desirable to use a stitch that's invisible from both sides. Pick up a single thread below the fold edge. Slip the needle in the fold for about

¼ inch (6 mm). Bring out needle and pick up a single thread below the fold. Again, slip needle in fold edge and continue in the same manner (See Fig. 10).

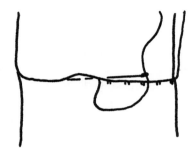

Figure 10

TAILORING EQUIPMENT

The well-equipped sewing center is a joy to the home sewer. To complete a successful tailoring job, such as a coat, these items of small sewing and pressing equipment are essential. Many of these items are not particularly expensive, and they can be found in the notions department of many fabric stores. And if you have a "handy" man in the family, you can get some of this equipment made for you.

PRESSING CLOTH

A satisfactory pressing cloth may be made from a piece of smooth-surfaced lightweight wool attached, with a seam, to a piece of medium weight muslin. Be sure to wash the muslin in hot sudsy water and rinse thoroughly to remove all sizing before using it as a press cloth! Lay the wool part of the pressing cloth against the woolen fabric during pressing. Dampen the muslin part and lay it over the wool pressing cloth to make steam when using a regular iron.

PRESSING HAM

An essential tool in pressing darts with nice, smooth ends is the pressing ham. All curved surfaces should be pressed over a ham. These are available in fabric stores, but you can make your own at home by stuffing pieces of oval shaped fabric with sawdust (See Fig. 11).

Figure 11

POINT PRESSER

A small wooden press board that is ideal to use for pressing seams open without getting seam marks on the right side is the point presser. This is a dandy gadget for that front jacket and facing seam. I always use it when working on collars and hard-to-get-to areas. If you press that tiny seam open before turning, it automatically pops out when turned (See Fig. 12).

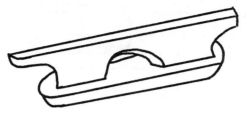

Figure 12

Pounding Block

Another item that is not too expensive but great for putting that good "finished" look into your garment. It's a small wooden block that is used to give the garment neat, thin edges. First, steam the area you are working in with a good, damp, press cloth. Then, lift the iron and edge of the cloth and give the garment edge a firm whack with the pounder. Presto! . . . a professional look. The base of some point pressers serves as a pounder also (See Fig. 13).

Figure 13

SLEEVE ROLL

Optional, but handy for opening those sleeve seams without making creases. It's much like a ham, but it's long and thin. You can substitute a rolled-up magazine covered with a turkish towel (See Fig. 14).

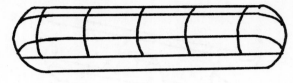

Figure 14

SLEEVE BOARD

Nice to have, but not essential. This is a press board which is like a miniature ironing board. This also can be used in pressing sleeve and other tubular seams (See Fig. 15).

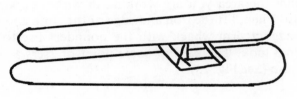

Figure 15

Of course you must have a steam iron (or use lots of water and a dry iron), a good pair of scissors for pocket openings and buttonholes, plus all of the obvious essentials. These include pins, needles, tracing paper, beeswax, and measuring tools. A well-informed sewing notions salesperson should be able to help you find these items you'll need if you don't have them on hand. If you can locate basting thread, it is a great help for all the tailor-basting we do in a jacket or coat—and it doesn't knot, a rarity among threads today.

One last, inexpensive, indispensable item: a piece of *tailor's chalk*. You'll use it often!

2

Women's Coats and Suits

Tailoring a coat or suit is reaching the highest point in your clothing construction experience. Tailoring need not be a frightening idea once you are familiar with the basic techniques in this manual.

The method of tailoring presented uses both traditional and simplified techniques. Your fabric and time will determine which method is best for you.

The keys to success in tailoring are ACCURATE CUTTING and MARKING, STITCHING, and PRESSING. The hints given here will help you achieve good results in these parts of the work. As beginners or expert seamstresses, you can tailor professional and fashion-wise clothing easily and in a minimum of time. I want you to *enjoy* tailoring; I don't want you to consider it a tedious impossibility.

15

YOUR SHOPPING LIST

THE PATTERN

More often than not, the simple pattern in a coat or suit is smarter and better styled than a complicated pattern—and of course, it's much easier to sew. Choose a style that will look good on you and that you'll look forward to tailoring. If you aren't excited about your pattern when you begin, you won't be thrilled with the finished coat or jacket.

Buy your pattern in your dress pattern size. The necessary ease has been allowed in the pattern.

THE FABRIC

Medium weight woolens, such as flannel, tweed, and fleece, are easy to tailor because they take the shape of the garment readily. Woolen fabrics that have a soft, lightly napped surface do not show seam lines when pressed. Refer back to the section discussing fabric selection (p. 2) for more detail.

For the amount of material to buy, check the pattern envelope, noting the width of the fabric. Allow extra for matching plaids and for fabric with nap, as usually indicated on your pattern envelope.

THE INTERFACING

Use hair canvas, such as Hymo, for most coatings and suitings for the front, collar, and hems. Hair canvas is recommended because it is easily shaped over the body contours and because it is resilient. This helps preserve the shape and well-pressed look of the garment.

Hair canvas comes in several weights. The heavier inter-facings are best for use with heavy woolen fabrics, and the lighter interfacings are best for use with medium weight and lightweight woolens. Lay your fabric and interfacing together over your hand and see which weight gives the shape your pattern requires.

Buy about two full garment lengths of your interfacing for fronts, collar, and hems. If you have an exceptionally large collar, you may need more.

Choose a firmly woven cotton (unbleached muslin or a dis-ciplined or regulated cotton) for interfacing across the back. You will need about ½ yard of this fabric.

THE LINING

The choice of lining is determined by the weight and charac-ter of the fabric and by the silhouette of the garment. A crisp texture like taffeta is a good lining choice for a semi-fitted or flared effect. A lightweight silk, a rayon, or an acetate crepe are suitable for fitted styles or soft lightweight fabrics.

Don't skimp on the quality of your lining, for you want it to last the life of your garment. Buy the amount suggested on your pattern envelope, unless you will be making big changes in the suggested finished length of the garment. Most lining fabrics are purchased preshrunk, but I always recommend pressing with a good steam iron before cutting.

THREAD AND BUTTONS

You will probably use a couple of spools of matching thread for the general construction of your coat or jacket. If your fabric is heavy, you may want to use heavy-duty thread to give more stability to your seams. In addition, you'll need contrasting thread for basting. If you plan to topstitch, consider either silk or polyester buttonhole twist. Two strands of your regular thread works nicely for this also.

Decide on buttons at the same time you purchase your fabric, because bound buttonholes will be one of the first steps in tailoring your coat. You need to know the size of your button before you can begin on the buttonholes.

CUTTING AND MARKING

FITTING THE PATTERN

Make your personal pattern adjustments on your tailored garment as you normally do for any garment, paying special attention to the fit. Pin the bodice front and back pattern pieces together with the darts also pinned and check the following areas:

1. Length and location of shoulder seam
2. Width across bust and back
3. Point of dart in relation to bust point
4. Armseye location
5. Length of garment

Pin sleeve seam together and then pin marked top of sleeve or shoulder seam and check length and width of sleeve.

Make necessary adjustments on your pattern. If you are making a coat, it is best to try the pattern on over a dress.

If you are working on very expensive fabric or if you have made extensive alterations, you may feel more confident making up your garment in muslin first. Cut out only the main pattern pieces, and then transfer all markings—be sure to include grainlines, lapel roll, center front, and center back. Trim off hem and seam allowances along center front and lapels. Machine-baste together and try on.

CUTTING

Accuracy is the most important element in both cutting and marking. Your cutting accuracy depends to some extent on how you have laid your pattern on your fabric. It is a good idea to cut heavy fabrics on a single thickness to prevent shifting. Also, many plaids and stripes are more accurately matched if they are cut on a single thickness.

Cut accurately with long strokes. The cutting line becomes your guide line for stitching.

CUTTING LINING

Follow your pattern directions for cutting lining with a couple of changes. I always add ⅛ inch (3 mm) to all seams in the lining so that it doesn't fit into the garment too snugly. The body contours seem to absorb the lining and make the garment pull in some areas if you don't add this extra ⅛ inch (3 mm).

Also, for additional ease in a coat, a pleat of 1 inch (2.5 cm) should be allowed at center back. If there is a lining pattern, check to see if this ease is allowed. If it is *not* allowed, you can easily make this adjustment before cutting. Place center back on fold of fabric, allowing ½ inch (1.2 cm) for pleat at center back edge and tapering to nothing at lower edge (See Fig. 16 for placement of pattern in order to allow for additional ease.)

Figure 16

CUTTING INTERFACING

There are two ways to cut interfacings. In suits and some coats a minimum type is used. With this type, the interfacing extends into the sleeve seam as most patterns instruct. The back neck interfacing is cut from the back neck facing pattern with ½ inch (1.2 cm) added on the lower outer edge. The only time I recommend using this *minimum* interfacing is when certain seams in the garment design prevent using more extensive interfacing (See Fig. 17).

Figure 17

For a good fit and a professional tailored look, I prefer the use of the more extensive interfacings. Use your pattern front to cut this interfacing, and mark it as follows (See Fig. 18):

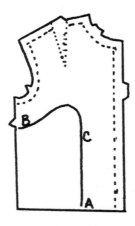

Figure 18

at A—width of facing pattern at lower edge

at B—3 inches (7.6 cm) below armhole at side seams

at C—just below bustline, the width of facing at lower edge.

Next, starting at lower edge, measure out ½ inch (1.2 cm) beyond width of facing and from this mark draw a line to B, curving from C to B and keeping the line ½ inch (1.2 cm) beyond the marks at those points.

Lay this pattern on your chosen interfacing fabric, and on the same grain as the garment front, and cut.

Back Interfacing

Using the garment back pattern, mark as shown in Figure 19:

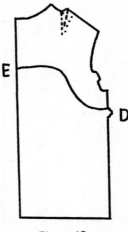

Figure 19

at D—3 inches (7.6 cm) below armhole at side seam

at E—4 (10.2 cm) to 6 (15.2 cm) inches below neckline

Then draw a curved line from the center back to the side seam as shown. Cut these extended interfacings on the same grain as the garment back from muslin or similar fabric.

Collars

Collar interfacings are cut from hair canvas or from other interfacings used in the front. With a notched collar, use the undercollar pattern and cut on the *bias* for best results. Follow your pattern directions for most different styles.

MARKING

Marking may be done with one of several methods, depending on your fabric.

TRACING WHEEL: The fastest, most accurate, and easiest way to mark most fabrics is with a tracing wheel and dressmaker's carbon. There is some danger that the carbon may show through to the right side on some fabrics, so it is best to test it before using it on your garment fabric or lining. This method is not suitable for many nubby and bulky fabrics.

Mark by following the lines on the pattern with the carbon side of the paper on the wrong side of the fabric. Use the edge of a ruler to make straight lines. This is an excellent method to mark center front, roll line, and buttonhole placement on your front interfacing.

TAILOR'S CHALK AND PINS: This method can be used on almost all fabrics because the chalk marks are not permanent. Fold fabric with right sides together. Start at the innermost edge to be marked, and work toward the edge of the pattern. Stick small-headed, straight pins through the tissue and both fabric layers. With tailor's chalk, mark the pin points with a dot on both wrong sides of the fabric. After the pattern is removed, the dots may be joined with a chalk mark and ruler.

TAILOR'S TACKS: These can be used on almost every fabric, but they are best for bulky, spongy fabrics or for fabrics which mar easily. Work with a long, unknotted, double thread. Place tacks at dots on pattern.

Take a small stitch through the pattern and both fabric layers, leaving a thread end 1 inch long. Take a second stitch over the first, leaving a long loop. Cut thread, leaving a 1 inch (2.5 cm) end. Cut through the top of the loop. Remove the pattern very carefully to avoid pulling out the threads.

Separate the fabric layers, clipping the threads between layers in order to leave thread tufts on both layers.

PRESSING TIPS

It is important that you understand now that the professional look of your garment may be lost due to inadequate or improper pressing. Too little pressing gives an unfinished, homemade look. Too much pressing makes a garment look old before it has been worn. It may shrink out the ease needed in a garment and make it look skimpy. Poor pressing techniques may actually press wrinkles in instead of removing them.

METHODS FOR PRESSING WOOL

These methods apply specifically to wool, but they can be modified and adapted to practically any type of fabric used in a tailored garment.

1. Underpress—press from the underside during all stages of construction. Remove all pins to avoid imprints. Test a sample to make sure basting doesn't imprint before pressing over it.

2. Press each piece of the garment thoroughly before sewing together. If, after a dart or seam has been pressed open, the area around the pressed part looks bubbly, press the entire piece again. But do not press *unnecessarily*.

3. Use a wool pressing cloth to protect the right side of the wool from direct contact with iron or steam iron.

4. After each unit is pressed, allow it time to dry, but *never press wool completely dry*.

5. Use plenty of steam, and press lightly with the grain line. Never bear down with the iron during steaming.

6. Press on a padded wood board or on a firm ironing board for well-creased edges and in order to avoid seam marks.

7. "Deaden" seam allowances and dart allowances to make wool less bulky by beating with a pounding block. This method may also be used to flatten creased and/or bulky edges.

8. Shape garment while pressing. Press over a pressing ham for curved surfaces, such as shoulder, tops of sleeves, and bust. Avoid pressing flat, thereby shrinking out the fullness created by darts and other construction.

9. Brush fabric on right side while steaming in order to avoid press marks.

10. Press each seam before it is crossed with another. Begin by pressing each seam with the tip of the iron only, pressing exactly on the line of stitching and in the direction stitched.

11. In most materials, darts are clipped and then pressed open. Before you clip, be sure your garment fits.

12. Press all inside seams open before turning hems. Avoid ripple in hems by pressing from the lower edge up—*not* around.

13. Press the armhole with the seams together, but without folding the seam inside either the bodice or sleeve. After pressing the seam (which should be trimmed to ½ inch (1.2 cm) and clipped at intervals in the lower half), turn it into the sleeve where it goes naturally when you put your hand and arm into the coat.

CONSTRUCTION

Sewing the garment in units makes it easier to handle. It's best to plan your work so that detail on each garment piece is completed before it is attached to another piece. The following suggested plan of work should give you a good idea of how you will progress toward your completed garment. You will find that the detail work in the beginning, such as bound buttonholes and pockets, will take quite a bit of time. Progression will be much faster once these important details are completed.

PLAN OF WORK

Make the garment in units.

A. Front: Darts; joining interfacing to garment; baste-stitching; buttonholes and pockets
B. Back: Center back seam; darts; joining interfacing to garment
C. Undercollar: Interfacing; back seam; pad-stitching
D. Top collar and front facing: Shoulder and neckline seams
E. Lining: Sewing units; putting lining together.

Put the Garment Together

A. Shoulder and underarm seams
B. Collar to garment
C. Hem
D. Facing to garment
E. Sleeves to garment

Finishing the Garment

A. Pockets and buttonholes
B. Hems
C. Edgestitching
D. Shoulder pads and lining

There are now two approaches to tailoring: traditional and contemporary. Traditional methods involve building shape and structure into a garment with an emphasis on hand sewing and attention to details. *The contemporary approach, evolving from changing life styles, is quick and easy, employing time-saving techniques and substituting machine-stitching and the use of fusibles for handwork.* Both produce acceptable results. I always use the traditional approach when working with wool and wool-like fabrics. The contemporary method is better suited to polyester knits, although the traditional method works well with knits also. The approach *you* select will depend on your fabric, on the amount of time you are willing to devote to this project, and on the type of garment you are making.

Throughout this manual I will discuss both methods for various areas of your garment. Perhaps it would be helpful for you to read through and see the differences before making a choice.

GARMENT FRONT

DARTS

1. Stitch dart in outer fabric. Backstitch or tie threads to secure ends of darts.

2. Trim darts to seam allowance width if they are exceptionally wide.

3. Press darts open as far as trimmed and continue by pressing a box pleat to the point. This can be done by inserting a knitting needle into the point of dart.

4. To reduce the bulk of *interfacing* darts, make them as follows:
   a. Cut marked dart between slanted stitching lines.
   b. Overlap the stitching lines and pin in place.

c. Stitch, starting at wide end, down stitching line and zigzag at the point to reinforce (See Fig. 20).

d. Trim both cut edges of interfacing close to stitching.

Figure 20

JOIN INTERFACING TO GARMENT FRONT

A. For Applied Facings

1. Trim outer corners of interfacing as shown in Figure 21.

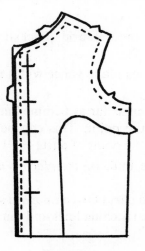

Figure 21

2. Pin interfacing to wrong side of front, matching centers and neckline, shoulder, and armhole edges.

3. Stay-stitch ½ inch (1.2 cm) from outer edge of front, neck, shoulders, and armholes. This line of stitching will later serve as a guide for the placement of twill tape.

4. Sew inner edge of interfacing in place just below the curve to the lower with a loose running stitch (See Fig. 22).

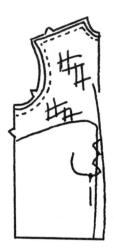

Figure 22

B. If Front Facing is cut in one with Front

1. At the fold line, clip the neckline seam and the lower edge.

2. Turn facing to inside and press lightly, making a slight crease along the fold.

3. With facing out flat, pin interfacing to wrong side of front along the crease and catch-stitch it along the edge. Also sew inner edge in place with long running stitches from curve to lower edge (See Fig. 23).

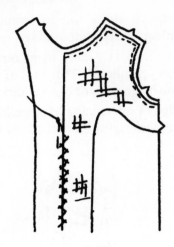

Figure 23

4. Stay-stitch around neckline, shoulder, and armhole seam line.

CONTEMPORARY METHOD

Fusible interfacing makes dart construction quite simple. Mark dart in outer fabric, but do not stitch. Cut out the dart in the interfacing and fuse in place, matching dart placement. Using cut edges as a guide, stitch dart (See Fig. 24).

Always cut the fusible on the grain indicated by the pattern piece (except for non-wovens, which have no grain). Trim seam allowances ½ inch (1.2 cm) and clip corners diagonally. This means that ⅛ inch (3 mm) of the interfacing will be caught in the seams.

On trimmed and turned seams, where area shaping is important, such as on the collar, cuffs, pockets, and flaps, trim

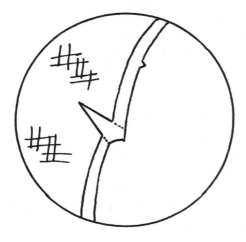

Figure 24

¾ inch (1.8 cm) off interfacing section. This means that the interfacing will stop ⅛ inch (3mm) before the seam line and will not be sewn into the seam (See Fig. 25).

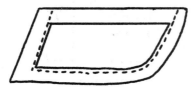

Figure 25

Fusible interfacings are applied to the wrong side of your garment fabric. Position interfacing exactly in place on garment section, the coated side of interfacing to the wrong side of fabric. Cover with a damp press cloth. Using a steam iron set at the fiber content of the interfacing, press for 8-10 seconds. Do not slide the iron back and forth. Lift and lower it to move to next section. Steam, heat, and pressure are essential to a good bond. Do not remove fabric from ironing board until cool.

BASTE-STITCHING

1. Hand-baste with running stitch the center front line and buttonhole locations. Use your markings on the interfacing as a guide line. The center front line will serve as a fitting guide later in construction.

2. For pockets that are set-in, baste-stitch pocket lines. Reinforce under pocket with a muslin strip 2 inches (5 cm) wide and ½ inch (1.2 cm) longer than finished pocket (See Fig. 26).

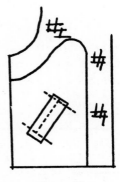

Figure 26

BUTTONHOLES

Bound buttonholes are usually found on all women's tailored garments. These are made while the garment section is still flat, after the interfacing has been applied. Machine-made buttonholes are stitched after the garment is completed.

In order to make a buttonhole, you must first know how large it needs to be. This is determined by the size and shape of your button. Pin a strip of woven seam binding around the fullest part of the button (do not include any shank). Remove strip, without unpinning, and measure from pin to fold. This measurement equals the proper length for your finished buttonhole.

Buttonholes are not difficult to make. However, like any skill, they take a bit of practice in order to achieve perfection. There are many methods to try. I will describe and illustrate two of those methods in this manual.

The most important aspect in making a buttonhole is *marking* carefully and accurately. The actual construction is quite simple, although again, perfection comes through practice.

1. Using dressmaker's carbon paper, mark buttonhole markings on interfacing as indicated by the pattern. These should include both cross-markings for buttonhole placement and the center front line.

2. Now, with a fine tip pen or a very sharp pencil, draw another vertical line ⅛ inch (3 mm) *outside* the center front line so that the buttons will rest on center front when buttoned. This line is the front edge of your buttonhole. From this line measure over the distance you need for your finished buttonhole (See Fig. 27).

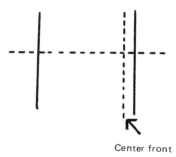

Center front

Figure 27

3. The width of the lips of your finished buttonhole is determined by the bulk of your fabric. Heavy fabrics need at least ³⁄₁₆ inch (4.7 mm) for each lip, while lighter fabrics (like double knits) require about ⅛ inch (3 mm) for each lip. Mark two horizontal lines, one above and the other below the buttonhole placement line, which indicate the desired width of your finished buttonhole lips. These lines will become your stitching lines when you begin making the actual buttonhole (See Fig. 28).

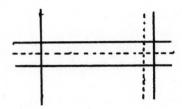

Figure 28

4. Baste-stitch through the center placement line of the buttonhole and check on the right side to see if it follows a crosswise grainline. You are now ready to make your buttonholes.

PATCH METHOD

1. Cut a straight grain lengthwise strip of fabric for each buttonhole 2 inches (5 cm) wide and 2 inches (5 cm) longer than the finished length of the buttonhole. You need one patch for each buttonhole.

2. Baste the patches *right sides together* over each buttonhole marking down the front garment edge. Push pins through from the back side of the garment to position each patch accurately.

3. Using about 18-20 stitches per inch, machine-stitch two parallel lines the exact length of the buttonhole (See Fig. 29).

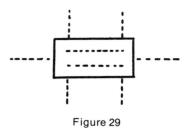

Figure 29

Stitch from the back side, using the markings on the interfacing as a guide. Secure thread endings.

4. From wrong side, start at center on marked line and slash through garment and patch to ⅜ inch (9 mm) from ends of stitching. Clip diagonally into corners (See Fig. 30).

Figure 30

5. Turn strip to wrong side through slash, pulling the ends to straighten. Form even lips and tack on the back side with a permanent basting stitch. On right side catch together the bound edges. (See Fig. 31).

Figure 31

6. Place garment right side up on sewing machine and fold material back so the end of patch and the triangular slashed piece can be put under the needle. Stitch and backstitch across strip, ends, and base of the triangular piece (See Fig. 32).

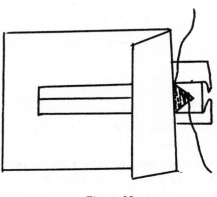

Figure 32

7. Steam buttonhole, remove basting, and resteam. If the buttonhole seems thick, pound with pounder after steaming. Finish underside of buttonholes later.

CONTEMPORARY WINDOW METHOD

Make Window

Use the marking method described for path buttonholes.

1. For each buttonhole, cut a piece of lining or underlining fabric the same color as garment, about 1½ inches (3.8 cm) wide and 1 inch (2.5 cm) longer than buttonhole. Center patch over buttonhole on right side, matching grainlines.

2. Using 18-20 stitches per inch, stitch a rectangle using your previously marked lines as a guide. Start stitching at the center of the buttonhole and overlap stitching when you have gone completely around the rectangle (See Fig. 33).

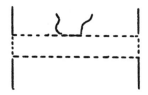

Figure 33

3. Slash between stitching lines from the center to within ⅜ inch (9 mm) of each end. Clip to the four corners, forming a triangle at each end. Do not clip through stitching.

4. Turn the fabric patch through slash to wrong side. Press fabric away from opening, forming a window. Make sure the patch does not show from the right side; this is the outer edge of the finished buttonhole (See Fig. 34).

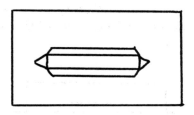

Figure 34

Make Lips

1. *Cut two straight pieces of garment fabric 1½ inches (3.8 cm) wide and 1 inch (2.5 cm) longer than the buttonhole. Cut stripes and plaids on the bias for a distinctive effect. Right sides together, baste the two pieces lengthwise through the center (See Fig. 35).*

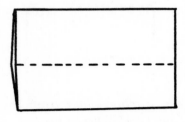

Figure 35

2. *Open pieces and refold wrong sides together; press.*

3. *Place lips behind window, with seam centered and excess at ends evenly divided.*

4. *Fold garment back, exposing seam. Using 18-20 stitches per inch, stitch over previous stitching through seam and lips. Extend stitching the entire length of fabric piece. Repeat on other side (See Fig. 36).*

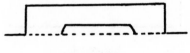

Figure 36

5. Stitch across each triangle end in the same manner. Press and pound to flatten edges. Remove basting after garment is completed.

OTHER BUTTONHOLE TIPS

If your fabric tends to ravel easily, a rectangle of fusible interfacing attached to the garment behind each buttonhole and to the back side of patch will help control raveling in the corners.

Cutting the fabric for the lips on the bias will give more flexibility to the lips. It also eliminates the need to match plaids or stripes in this area.

Always make a sample buttonhole before working on the buttonholes on your garment. This helps you decide which size lips look best, which length is best for your button, and how close you can clip to the corners without having them ravel.

POCKETS

There are hundreds of different kinds and shapes of pockets in women's coats and jackets. Follow your pattern instructions as a general rule, but there are a few tricks to making and attaching the following kinds.

IN-SEAM

When you sit down, in-seam pockets sometimes gap, exposing the pocket lining. You can eliminate this unsightly look by cutting the underside of the pocket lining from your outer garment fabric.

It is also a good idea to reinforce in-seam pockets, especially in stretchy fabrics, along what would be the seam line in the front section. Place edge of woven seam binding or ½ inch (1.2 cm) twill tape along the seam line with remainder towards pocket. Use a long running stitch through the center of the tape to hold it in place (See Fig. 37).

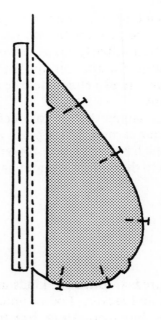

Figure 37

PATCH

The following method assures a finished, flat edge with no exposed lining. This pocket may be interfaced for body and for crisper edges in addition to being lined. Cut interfacing and trim off seam allowances and the area above fold line; catch-stitch or fuse in place. Press under pocket seam allowances. Trim hem seam allowance ¼ inch (6 mm) and notch any curves. Baste. Fold hem down and slipstitch ends to pocket.

Cut lining from pocket pattern minus the area above fold line. Press under seam allowances plus an extra ⅛ inch (3 mm), so that folded edges will be inside pocket edges. Press under upper edge so it overlaps hem edge by ½ inch (1.2 cm); trim excess to ½ inch (1.2 cm). Slipstitch lining to pocket (See Fig. 38).

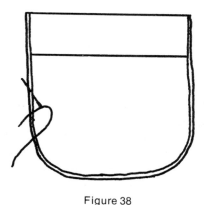

Figure 38

To attach patch pockets, drape garment over a tailor's ham and pin pocket in place. This method insures that the pocket will conform to the curve of the body when attached. Edge-stitch, slipstitch, or topstitch pockets in place.

FLAPS

It is rarely necessary to interface flaps. Always cut the under-side ⅛ inch (3 mm) smaller than the top piece in order to keep the edges rolled toward the body. Take great care to make sure that the flaps are stitched evenly. To get good corners on your flaps, always use small stitches and sew two stitches diagonally across the points. This will insure professional-looking corners when you turn the flaps (See Fig. 39).

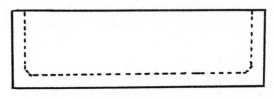

Figure 39

Use this method anywhere in the jacket where a good point is desired. It is a trick you can use to avoid little lumps at the corners. The diagonal stitching absorbs the excess fullness at the points and you end up with sharp, smooth, professional corners. After the flaps are stitched, trim closely, especially at the corners, and grade your seam allowances. Press that tiny seam open with the point presser, turn, and press again.

TAPING AND PAD STITCHING

Cotton twill tape is used in a tailored garment as a reinforcement to preserve a measurement or shape that will service hard wear, such as the roll line of a lapel. You can also shape the curved bottom edge which is in some jackets with taping.

Tape is enclosed in the front seam of women's coats to keep that well-handled edge from stretching out of shape. When there is no lapel in the design, simply enclose one edge of ¼ inch (6 mm) twill tape in the front seam and catch-stitch the inside edge to the interfacing (See Fig. 40).

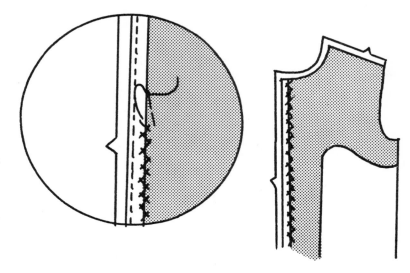

Figure 40

Tape the shoulder seams in the same way.

The lapel area is one of the most important areas to shape in a tailored garment. It sets the shape of the garment front and is very influential in how the collar rolls. For this reason, the roll line is defined and preserved by taping and pad-stitching.

Prepare the front section by attaching the interfacing as described before, except leave the lapel area free when stitching the layers together. Using ⅜ inch (9 mm) wide tape, start 2 inches (5 cm) above the buttonhole area on the canvas and end an inch before the neck seam. Place the tape *behind* the marked roll line of both canvas fronts. This tape should be pulled slightly as you apply it in order to control the bias and keep the lapels flat on the chest. Anchor the tape with small running stitches. Try to catch only the canvas and tape, but be sure to use matching thread in case you catch the outer fabric. Be sure you use the same amount of tape for both canvases so that your fronts will be identical. I usually cut the tape ½-1 inch (1.2 cm-2.5 cm) shorter than the roll line.

Now catch-stitch each side of the tape to the canvas with ½ inch (1.2 cm) stitches (See Fig. 41).

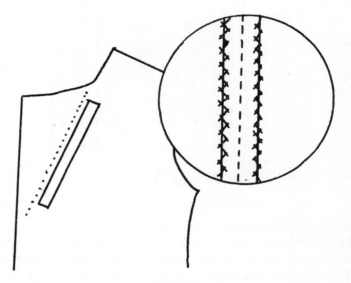

Figure 41

To pad-stitch lapel, roll it over your hand and hold it as it will be worn. Use thread in the same color as your fabric. Make rows of pad-stitching ⅜ inch (9 mm) apart and parallel to the roll line, working back and forth through all layers. Always keep the lapel rolled in the same position. When near the point of the lapel, make the stitches shorter and the rows closer together in order to make the point firmer and to insure that the lapel point will roll toward the garment (See Fig. 42).

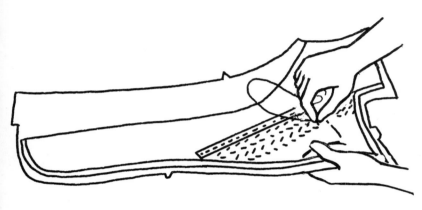

Figure 42

CONTEMPORARY LAPEL ROLL

To achieve a lapel roll the unstructured way, use two layers of a fusible interfacing, plus a length of ¼ inch (6 mm) twill tape. Cut front interfacing and fuse in place. This is one interfacing layer. For the second layer, cut a triangle of fusible interfacing to fit the lapel point only. Trim away all seam allowances and clip point diagonally so none of this second layer will be caught in the seam. Fuse the triangle on top of the front interfacing between the seam lines at the lapel point. This triangle helps weight the lapel point so it will always fall toward the garment.

Cut the twill tape the length of the roll line minus 1 inch (2.5 cm). The lapel roll line begins at the neck seam and ends where the seam line and the roll line intersect.

Mark the lapel roll line on the front interfacing. Position the twill tape ¼ inch (6 mm) from the roll line toward the body of the garment. Pin one end of the tape ½ inch (1.2 cm) from the lower end of the roll line; pin the other end of the tape at the neck seam where the lapel roll line begins. Pin the tape in place so the fabric is eased evenly. Stretching the tape as you stitch, zigzag through the middle or stitch on both sides of the tape through all layers. This stitching will be hidden by the finished lapel. Because the tape is shorter than the roll line, the lapel is encouraged to roll beautifully (See Fig. 43).

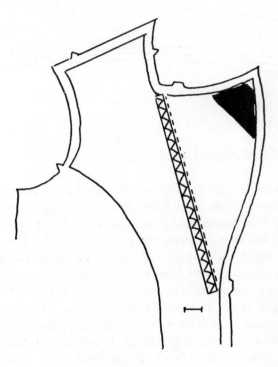

Figure 43

GARMENT BACK

1. Stitch center back seam if your garment has one.

2. Stitch shoulder darts in garment fabric.

3. Trim darts in garment to width of seam allowance if wider. Press darts open as on fronts.

4. Lap interfacing darts, stitch, and trim.

5. Press entire back section and interfacing.

6. Join interfacing to garment (See Fig. 44).

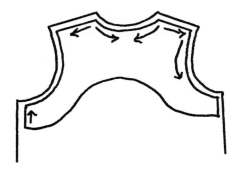

Figure 44

   a. Stay-stitch coat and interfacing together as on fronts.

   b. Trim corners at seam ends and trim interfacing close to stay-stitching.

Now is the time to join the fronts to the back and to do the first initial fitting. It's finally beginning to look like a coat or jacket. Pay special attention to the fit at the neckline, as the collar will be your next area of attention.

COLLAR

The idea in tailoring a collar is to permanently shape the undercollar and then attach the upper collar. The upper collar then takes on the shape of the undercollar when the two are joined.

UNDERCOLLAR

1. Stitch center back seam in undercollar and press open.

2. Cut interfacing from undercollar pattern, making sure that it is also cut on the bias to allow proper shaping.

3. Join center backs of interfacing by overlapping seam lines, stitch, and then trim close to stitching.

4. Pin interfacing to wrong side of undercollar, and cut out corners diagonally to reduce bulk.

Marking the Roll Line

Many patterns already have a roll line marked on the undercollar pattern, and you can use this as an easy guide. If it is not marked on your pattern, you can find it by pinning the collar onto your garment, starting at center back. Pin right side of undercollar to wrong side of garment at neck edge, matching seam lines. Hand baste in place. Try garment on and pin front edges closed at top button. Don't forget that ⅝ inch (1.5 cm), for the seam, will eventually be removed.

Roll collar into a position that frames the neck. If there are lapels, the collar should form a smooth line with them. Have someone mark the roll line with pins and then mark roll line with hand-basting before removing pins.

Pad-stitching: Method A

Pad-stitching not only sets the roll, it molds the undercollar into its permanent shape. The stitch used in pad-stitching is a tiny slanted basting stitch. (Refer back to section on Tailoring Stitches.) Work in rows and take a tiny horizontal stitch through all layers of fabric, catching only a thread or two of your outer garment fabric. Repeat stitch directly below the first, spacing stitches ¼-½ inch (6 mm-1.2 cm) apart. The first row should be directly along the roll line; then work toward the inner edge of the collar, making rows parallel to the roll line. As you sew, roll the collar over your fingers, positioning it as it will be worn, in order to shape the roll.

To pad-stitch beyond the roll line, begin at center back. Stitches may be a little longer here, and you should follow the grainline of the interfacing. Work toward the collar points, but don't go beyond seam line. Trim interfacing close to stitching on outer and side edges (See Fig. 45).

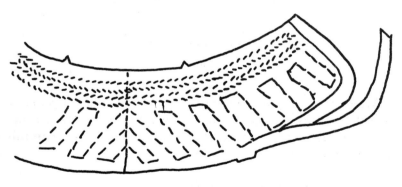

Figure 45

Trim any corners in garment fabric diagonally almost to the seam line and fold all seam allowances to the wrong side. Baste close to folded edge. Press to get sharp edges, clipping or notching curves if necessary. Trim folded edges to ⅜ inch (9 mm).

Steam press the undercollar by placing it around a ham (See Fig. 46).

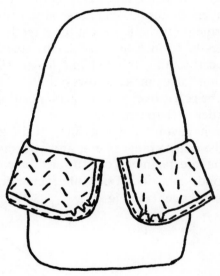

Figure 46

After pressing, pin the front edges of the collar together so the collar forms a circle. Keep it in this position until you set it into your garment, or you will lose the shape you carefully stitched and pressed in.

Undercollar—Contemporary Method

When using a fusible interfacing, cut a second piece of fusible interfacing which will fit the undercollar from roll line to neck seam edge. Cut this on the true bias and place the center back on the fold to eliminate the bulk of another seam. Fuse this second layer over the trimmed and pressed center back collar seam. (See Fig. 47.) Fold undercollar along roll line, interfacing side out. Steam press to shape with the undercollar curved around and pinned to a ham. Make sure the piece is completely dry before removing.

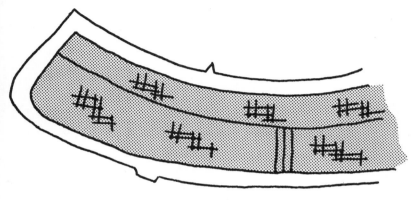

Figure 47

ATTACHING COLLAR

Stitch back and front facings together at the shoulder seams and press. Stitch facings to coat fronts, stopping at pattern marking (usually a large dot) indicating where collar ends. The marking will be at the top of the lapel, if the coat has a lapel. Clip seam allowance at end of stitching.

Attaching Collars to Garment: Method A

Grade seam allowances, trim bulk from corners, and notch curves. Turn facing inside and press, making sure the seam edges roll slightly to the underside. Steam and pound to get nice, sharp edges. Baste neck edges together (See Fig. 48).

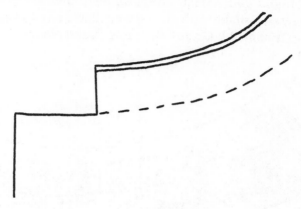

Figure 48

Stitch ½ inch (1.2 cm) from the edge on the outer and side edges of the upper collar. Turn under these edges so the stitching is hidden underneath. Hand baste close to folded edges and press with steam and pounder to get the sharpest edges possible (See Fig. 49).

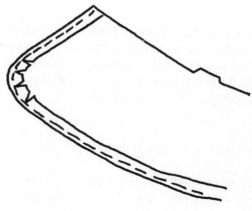

Figure 49

Pin upper collar to facing and neck edges with the *right* side of the collar to the *wrong* side of the garment, edges even. Clip coat neck edge wherever necessary in order to match markings exactly. Make sure the ends of the collar reach to the end of the clipped seam allowances of the lapels. Machine-stitch through all layers (See Fig. 50).

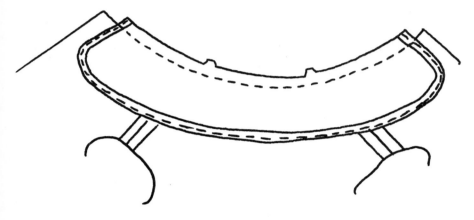

Figure 50

Press seam allowances toward the collar. Trim and grade seam allowances so the longest layer is next to the upper collar.

Pin undercollar to upper collar, *wrong* sides together. Holding collars in wearing position, baste together, matching center back seam of undercollar and center back seam of jacket. Overlap upper collar edge slightly beyond undercollar edge to prevent seam from showing when collar is worn. Hand-sew outer folded edges of undercollar to upper collar with a felling stitch, placing stitches about ⅛ inch (3 mm) apart. Slipstitch collar at neck edge of jacket. Now you have a professional-looking collar with sharp, clearly defined edges! (See Fig. 51).

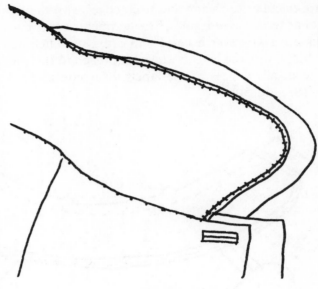

Figure 51

Pad-Stitching: Method B

Mark pad-stitching lines on interfacing following straight of grain (using both lengthwise and crosswise grain), one inch apart and only to the seam lines (See Fig. 52).

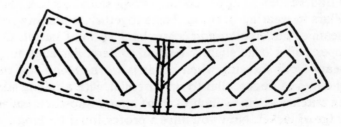

Figure 52

Machine-stitch on interfacing side, working from the middle toward each end.

To give the undercollar a good fitting curve, shape it on a ham. Fold nearly in half at center back, tapering to seam line at ends. Mold half at a time, using the steam iron lightly. Fold larger collars about ⅓ at center back for better curve.

Attaching Collars to Garment: Method B

To stitch undercollar to garment, first clip neck edge to stay-stitching about every ½ inch (1.2 cm). With right sides together, pin undercollar to coat, matching markings exactly. Stitch exactly to, not beyond, the seam line of the undercollar. Back-stitch at both ends. Clip curves and press seam open over a tailor's ham. Whipstitch the seam allowance of the undercollar to the interfacing to keep the seam allowance flat (See Fig. 53).

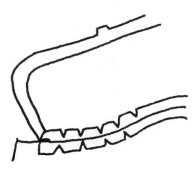

Figure 53

Join front and back facings at shoulder seams; stay-stitch neck edge, clip to stay-stitching. Sew upper collar to facings between markings at neck edge. Trim seam, clip curves, and press over a tailor's ham. Make sure the front edges of the upper collar are exactly equal. If not, adjust the upper collar at the neck seam (See Fig. 54).

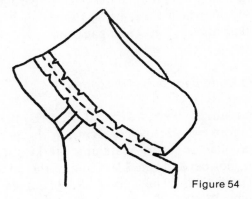

Figure 54

Pin facing and upper collar to garment and undercollar, matching markings. Stitch in the following sequence:

1. Stitch around the collar, starting and ending exactly at the neck seam; it is better to stop a little short than to go beyond the marking where the collar joins the front facing or lapel (See Fig. 55).

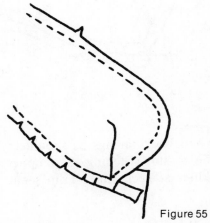

Figure 55

2. Stitch from the neck seam around the lapel, if any, and down the front of the garment to the hem. Repeat for the other side (See Fig. 56).

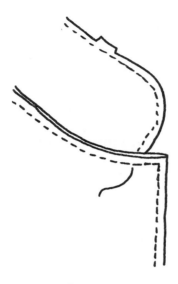

Figure 56

Before trimming any of these seams, turn the collar and facings to the inside and check to see if the collar and facing/lapel will lie perfectly flat. If it puckers, one of the stitchings, either on the collar or the facing/lapel went a stitch or two over the corner markings. If this happens, remove the extra stitches. If the lapel does not form a smooth, even line with the collar seam, the stitching of the lapel did not coincide exactly with the collar stitching. Remove the stitching of the lapel and stitch again at the seam line.

Trim seams and clip corners. Clip curves. Grade seams on the collar and facings. This grading will reverse itself at the roll line if the garment has a lapel. You will also find that the upper collar is slightly larger than the undercollar, allowing it to roll slightly over the undercollar and cover the seam at the edge.

Catch-stitch upper collar seam allowances to undercollar seam allowance between shoulder seams.

FINISHING BACK OF BUTTONHOLES

Two methods are given for finishing the buttonhole on the facing side.

METHOD A

Adjust the facing of the garment and baste by hand into permanent position around the buttonholes. Stab pins through the facing from the right side of your garment at each end of the buttonhole opening. The two pins should follow a grain line. Slit the facing between the pins. Turn the raw edges under and whipstitch in place. Make your stitches very close together so the edge will not ravel out (See Fig. 57).

Figure 57

If you are using this method, wait until the lining is inserted before finishing the back of your buttonholes.

METHOD B

This method produces a neat bound buttonhole in the facing. It is simple to make with no frayed edges around the facing side of the buttonhole. Accuracy in marking is a must!

Adjust the facing of the garment and pin into permanent position. From the right side of the garment, mark with pins through on the facing the length of each buttonhole, then carefully baste each buttonhole on the wrong side of the facing.

1. Cut true bias facings from lining fabric 1½ inches (3.8 cm) wide and 1 inch (2.5 cm) longer than the buttonhole to be faced.
   a. Cover each buttonhole length on the facing with the bias fabric with right sides of materials together.
   b. Stitch, from the facing side, a rectangle around marked buttonholes, making sure that it is the exact size of the buttonhole to be faced.
   c. Cut through the buttonhole length to within ¾₁₆ inch (4.8 mm) of ends, then diagonally out to corners (See Fig. 58).

2. Pull bias through the rectangular opening to wrong side of the garment, fold along stitching line, baste, and press.

3. This opening is fitted to the wrong side of the buttonhole, basted, and closely slipstitched into position *after* the lining is inserted. Steps 1 and 2 are completed *before* insertion of the lining.

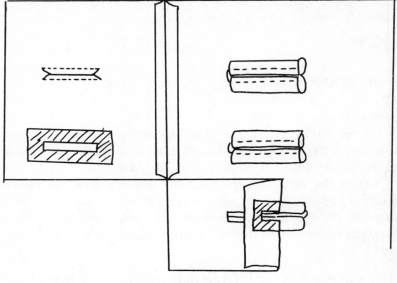

Figure 58

SLEEVES

DARTS

Stitch and press elbow darts, if your pattern has them, down toward sleeve hem.

Many patterns have a two-piece sleeve, consisting of an upper sleeve and an under sleeve. Stitch seams of sleeve sections, easing upper sleeve to fit under sleeve between markings. Press both seams over a sleeve roll.

EASING SLEEVE INTO GARMENT

The ease must be put in the correct spot if you want the sleeve to feel comfortable and look well. To control ease, put a row of 8-10 stitches per inch on the ⅝ inch (1.5 cm) seam line, stitching between notches across the top of the sleeve. With a thinner fabric, another line of long stitches should be placed ⅜ inch (9 mm) from the edge.

Gather sleeve to fit armhole loosely. Shrink extra fullness from seam allowance over pressing ham or small end of ironing board (See Fig. 59).

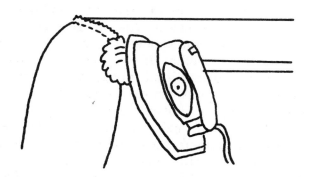

Figure 59

Holding sleeve toward you, pin it into your garment, matching underarm seams, notches, dots at mid-front and mid-back, and the marking at the top of the sleeve. Adjust fullness between these markings, pinning carefully on the seam line. If you are unsure about the fit, baste the sleeve in place and try your garment on. Otherwise, machine-stitch from sleeve side, exactly on the ⅝ inch (1.5 cm), using a machine-basting stitch.

After checking fit, stitch again ½ inch (1.2 cm) from the edge for reinforcement. It is difficult to get inside a lined garment to restitch a sleeve seam which has pulled loose after wear.

Trim the entire seam to ½ inch (1.2 cm), and then retrim underarm area from notch to notch down to ⅜ inch (9 mm).

Lightly press seam toward sleeve. Be careful not to overpress in this area.

SHOULDER PADS

Shoulder pads are not always used in women's garments, but they do add to the shaping of your garment—and they do protect your garment on the hanger. You can use them to disguise figure faults, such as round shoulders, thin shoulders, or one shoulder higher than the other. If you decide to use them, you should have them in place for all fittings. You can buy ready-made shoulder pads, or it is very easy to make your own out of polyester fleece. Pin your front and back pattern pieces together on the shoulder seam to make your pattern. Make a tissue pattern, using the armhole curve from notch to notch and another curve drawn approximately 1 inch (2.5 cm) from the neck edge. Cut graduated layers of polyester fleece and stab-stitch together until the desired shape and height has been achieved (See Fig. 60).

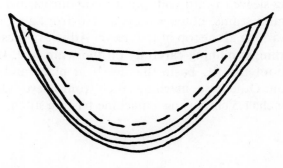

Figure 60

With the garment on, position shoulder pads in preparation for sewing. The pad should extend ⅜ inch (9 mm) beyond the armhole seam. Pin from the outside, then baste. Turn garment inside out and slipstitch pad to sleeve seam allowance. Tack point of pad to shoulder seam allowances.

SLEEVE HEAD

A heading can be sewn into the sleeve to support the weight of the shoulder cap. The heading does not take the place of a shoulder pad, but is sewn in after the shoulder pad.

Cut a strip of lamb's wool or polyester fleece 3 inches (7.6 cm) wide and 6 inches (15.2 cm) long for each sleeve. Make a 1 inch (2.5 cm) fold on one long edge. Slipstitch folded edge of padding along seam at cap of sleeve with widest part next to the sleeve (See Fig. 61).

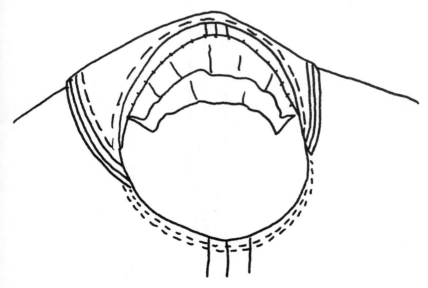

Figure 61

HEMS

It is usually easier to have your hems completed before you set in the lining. Try your garment on and have the hem marked accurately. Press a crease with the steam iron exactly on this hem line. Trim hem to an even width all around, usually no wider than 2½ inches (6.4 cm) and no narrower than 2 inches (5 cm).

Mark long sleeve hems so that they cover the wrist bone. The method for attaching interfacing and hemming is exactly the same as for the lower hem, except that the finished hem width should be about 1½ inches (3.8 cm).

Remove bulk in hem by trimming seam allowances to ¼ inch (6 mm) (See Fig. 62).

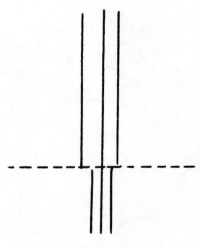

Figure 62

Cut a true bias strip of interfacing 1 inch (2.5 cm) wider than your hem allowance. Place the interfacing on the wrong side of your garment with the lower edge extending ½ inch (1.2 cm) below hemline. Baste to hemline with long running stitches. Sew upper edge of interfacing to garment or underlining with a catch-stitch (See Fig. 53). If you press a crease in the lower edge of your interfacing before inserting it in the hem, it is easy to lay both creases together for correct positioning.

To reduce bulk in front facing area, trim hem allowance to ½ inch (1.2 cm), as shown in Figure 63. Turn up hem and hold in place with long running stitches through hem and interfacing only. An alternate method is to catch-stitch the hem to the interfacing.

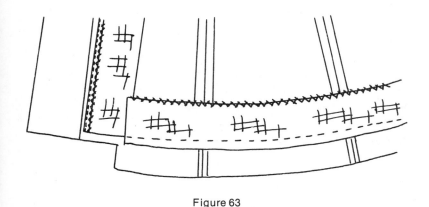

Figure 63

The interfacing extending below the hemline will provide a soft rolled effect. Fold facing back in place and slipstitch hem at lower edge. Catch-stitch raw edge of facing to hem allowance.

Press hem lightly.

CONTEMPORARY METHOD

Cut bias strips of fusible interfacing ½ inch (1.2 cm) wider than hem allowance. Place on wrong side of garment with one edge on fold line of hem and remainder into the body of the garment. Cut at seams and place under seam allowances, not on top. Fuse in place. Turn up hem and hold in place with long running stitches through hem and interfacing only.

Before using this method, make sure that the fusible interfacing will not make a ridge on the right side of your garment. Always test a sample before proceeding.

TRIM STITCHING

Often a tailored garment will not be improved with a trimstitching of hand-picking or topstitching. A garment sometimes has a finer quality look without them. On the other hand, many garments are improved a great deal by the addition of trim stitching. Try either method for a few inches on the edges of your garment before making a decision.

TOPSTITCHING

Set gauge or quilting foot at ⅜ to ½ inch (9 mm-1.2 cm). Stitch front of garment and collar edge in a continuous row. Follow your pattern directions for a notched collar.

Use either two strands of polyester thread or silk buttonhole twist for the best appearance. Your machine stitch length should be longer than normal, usually around 8 stitches per inch. Always hand-baste the area to be topstitched in order to prevent creeping or distortion while stitching.

Pound area with clapper before and after topstitching is done.

HAND-PICKING

Hand-picking is done ⅜ to ¾ inch (9 mm-1.8 cm) from edges depending on fabric and style of garment. It is done by hand with single buttonhole twist or cotton embroidery thread. The stitch must go through the interfacing and need not go all the way through the underside of the garment. The space on the top side is about ¼ inch (6 mm) between pickings.

After making stitches for several inches, wrap the thread around your finger and pull the thread firm to lie straight in the garment. Reverse the stitches at the lapel roll. Pound with clapper before and after hand-picking is done.

LINING

PRESSING BEFORE LINING IS ATTACHED

Allow time for both garment and lining to dry completely after the necessary additional pressing. Careful handling while making the coat or jacket can reduce this to a minimum.

Press lining on the underside. Test iron temperature on a scrap of lining fabric before pressing. Test for effects of steam on your lining, too.

Sleeve

Place lower sleeve hem on sleeve board or sleeve roll. Steam press and use clapper for creased edges. Place top of sleeve over pressing ham. Steam, shape, and brush. Do not press creases in sleeves.

Shoulder Seams

Place on top of pressing ham. Steam, shape, and brush.

Neckline

Place lapel over top of ham with the facing side up. Press body of lapel, not the edge. Remove and pull gently along line of roll while still steaming. This helps set the roll of the lapel. Never press a crease line along lapel or collar.

Bustline

Place over pressing ham, steam, and brush.

Body of Garment

Place on regulation ironing board. Press side seams from lower edge toward sleeve in the direction they were stitched. Steam, use clapper at hem edge, and brush along seams and body of garment. Dry thoroughly on hanger.

PUTTING IN LINING

The lining may be sewn into your garment by sewing machine or by hand. Machine-sewing gives a sturdy finish; hand-sewing gives a custom finish.

BY MACHINE

This is a ready-to-wear technique used on jackets, coats, and children's clothing.

Finish the garment completely except for slipstitching the facings to the buttonholes. Construct the lining, including setting in the sleeves.

With right sides together, pin lining to the facings, matching center backs and shoulder seams. Stitch, starting 3 inches (7.6 cm) above lower edge of one front facing and continuing around the neckline to within 3 inches (7.6 cm) of the lower edge on the opposite side of the garment. Press seam allowances toward the lining (See Fig. 64).

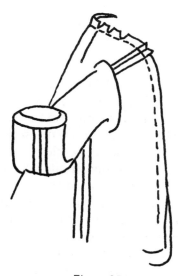

Figure 64

Try jacket or coat on and place pins through the garment and lining fabrics around the waist level. Take off garment and lay on table. Smooth lining down from pins and turn under lining hem so it is 1 inch (2.5 cm) shorter than your coat or jacket.

Coat linings are hemmed separately by turning under lining hem allowance and hemming with a slipstitch.

Ease must be allowed in a jacket lining because it is hemmed directly to the jacket hem, and you want to prevent the bottom edge of the jacket from pulling up. Turn under jacket lining so that it is 1 inch (2.5 cm) shorter than the jacket; crease it in this position. Then, push crease up so that it lies 1½ inches (3.8 cm) above bottom edge of jacket and slipstitch it in place. Allow this ½ inch (1.2 cm) tuck to fall down naturally and slipstitch last 3 inches (7.6 cm) along facing.

Turn the lining right side out. Insert sleeve linings into sleeve. Tack seams of lining to garment seams at underarm seam. Hem sleeve linings, allowing ease as you did at the jacket's bottom edge.

BY HAND

Stay-stitch armhole areas ½ inch (1.2 cm) from edge; neckline and front edges ⅝ inch (1.5 cm) from edge. All darts should be made and pressed in the same direction as in the garment. At center back, press pleat to one side. Working from the right side of the lining, catch-stitch the back pleat for about 1½ inches (3.8 cm) at neckline. Stitch shoulder and side seams; press.

On the front and back neckline edges, clip seam allowances to stay-stitching on curves. Press seam allowances to wrong side, rolling stay-stitching line slightly under so that it will not show. Press under ½ inch (1.2 cm) at lower edge of lining.

It should be noted that the hem in a jacket or coat is more easily finished after the lining is installed in the garment.

Turn garment wrong side out and match the center back pleat of the lining to center back of neckline facing and pin. Match the side seams of the lining to garment seams at underarm seam and pin.

Turn the lining away from the garment. Pin one side seam allowance of the lining to the corresponding side seam allowance of the garment. Tack loosely with long running stitches, starting 2 inches (5 cm) below the armhole and stitching for about 5 inches (12.7 cm) (See Fig. 65).

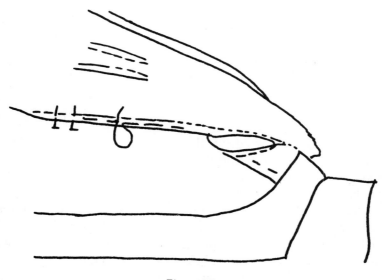

Figure 65

Lap and pin the turned edge of lining over the facing, matching raw edges. Sew the lining to facings with small hemming stitches, easing the lining slightly over the bust. Sew to within 3 inches (7.6 cm) of the garment hemline on both sides (See Fig. 66).

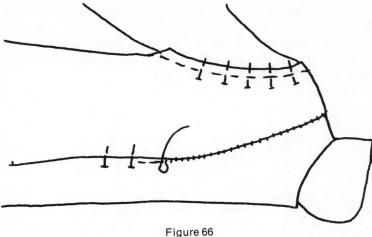

Figure 66

Pin the bottom fold of the lining over the jacket hem, matching raw edges. Smooth the excess length in the lining up from the hem and baste or pin the lining to the jacket about 3 inches (7.6 cm) above the hem, below the fullness.

Slipstitch lining hem in place. The extra length in the lining will automatically fall down over the hem. This ease prevents the lining from pulling the garment up on the inside and makes wearing the garment more comfortable (See Fig. 67).

Remove basting or pins; sew the lower front 3 inches (7.6 cm) of the lining to the facings. Lightly press the lining.

Prepare sleeve lining with ease around the top cap the same way you did the garment sleeve. Press hem edges under ½ inch (1.2 cm).

Turn the garment and lining sleeves wrong side out. Pin one seam allowance of the lining to the corresponding seam allowance of the sleeve, matching notches and keeping the top edges even. Sew seam allowances together loosely with a long, running stitch, starting and ending about 3 inches (7.6 cm) from top and bottom of sleeve (See Fig. 68).

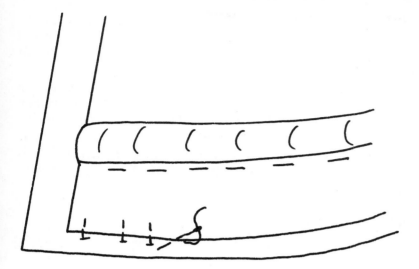

Figure 67

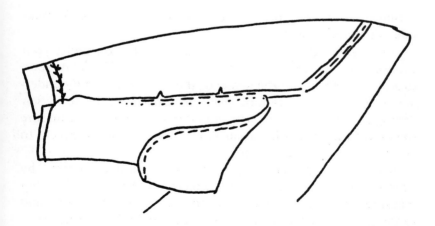

Figure 68

Slip your hand down inside the sleeve lining from the arm-hole. Grasp the lower edge of the garment sleeve and lining and draw them through the lining, turning the lining right side out over the garment sleeve.

Pin lining sleeve to armhole, matching markings. Draw up the ease threads in top of lining from both ends. Distribute ease evenly, fitting the lining over sleeve. Turn under the edge of the lining on the seam line and pin. Place pins perpendicular to the seam line. Sew in place with very small hemming stitches. This is an area of great stress, so make these stitches close together. You may even want to go around twice.

Attach sleeve lining hem, using the method described for jacket lining hem.

FINISHING TOUCHES

Slipstitch the openings on the back of the facing to the back-side of the buttonholes.

It is a good idea to add a reinforcement button under your fashion button if it will receive heavy strain, or if it will be sewn to a fragile fabric. On the inside of the garment, directly under-neath the button location, place a small, flat button. Sew through the button when attaching the outer button, being sure to sew over another object, such as a match or a toothpick, to allow for a shank (See Fig. 69).

You can blend snaps right into your finished garment by covering them with fabric. Cut two circles of lining fabric that measure twice the diameter of the snap. Make small hand running stitches around the edge of each circle. Do not fasten or

Figure 69

break thread. Place the hole snap section face down in center of circle. Then pull up the thread and secure with several stitches. Repeat for the second section, snapping and unsnapping sections to bring the ball through the fabric before pulling up thread. Sew as usual to your garment (See Fig. 70).

Figure 70

Use French tacks 1 or 2 inches (2.5 cm-5 cm) long to join hem of lining to hem of coat at side seams and at center back. Take loose stitches between the two fabric pieces and work blanket stitch over the threads (See Fig. 71).

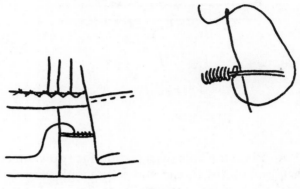

Figure 71

Or, use four strands of your thread and work a single crochet for 1 or 2 inches (2.5 cm-5 cm) between lining and coat hems to anchor them in place.

Use catch-stitch to cover raw edge of coat or jacket facing as shown in Figure 72.

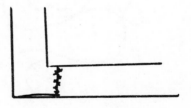

Figure 72

3

Men's Jackets and Pants

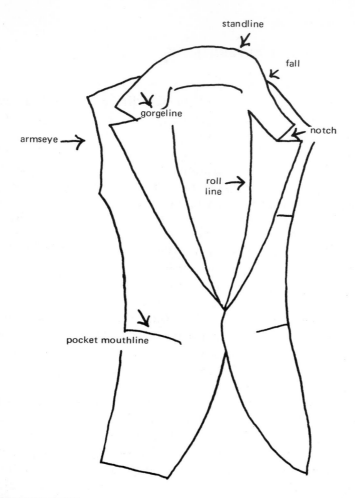

standline

fall

gorgeline

notch

armseye

roll
line

pocket mouthline

TERMINOLOGY

This illustration should help you become familiar with the terminology that I will be using throughout this part of *Tailoring the Easy Way*. Specific areas of the jacket can be more easily recognized by use of the proper terms.

DESIGNING AND ALTERATIONS

We can take advantage of the well-drafted and well-designed patterns in our stores and still make changes and adaptations to suit our own particular man.

When you purchase a jacket pattern, use his chest measurement. If he needs an odd number size (patterns come in even numbered sizes), I suggest you buy the next larger size—and then take generous seams when sewing.

Regardless of what you've chosen in the way of pattern and fabric, I always recommend that you make a muslin shell to check fit. You can use an old sheet or any fabric that has no give. This is the easiest way to see any problems quickly.

Here's the best way to make the muslin mock-up from your pattern. Cut the jacket out of muslin (or whatever) but do not include facings or upper collar. Mark the center fronts and roll lines of the lapels with a tracing wheel. Then, sew the entire jacket in machine-basting stitches. Cut off all hems on sleeves and bottom of the jacket. Set in the sleeves and put on only the undercollar for accurate fit.

The best guide to use in fitting this muslin is common sense. Men have fewer curves than women, so you should have fewer fitting problems. Remember that this muslin mock-up is used for working out any problems. Custom tailors simply make obvious necessary allowances for body variations—more fabric where an individual may need it, and less fabric where a man tends to be slimmer.

Here are some check points to look for: length of jacket, width of jacket, fit of collar, armhole comfort, and length of sleeves.

Men often complain about the snug underarm area when they first try on the muslin. Usually this is true because the area is not clipped and there is no give to the muslin. Also, there is no slippery lining to ease that shirt sleeve through. So, unless this area really binds him, it almost certainly won't need to be altered at this time. However, if this tightness is too uncomfortable, you can add fabric to the back seams of the jacket and the sleeves (See Fig. 73).

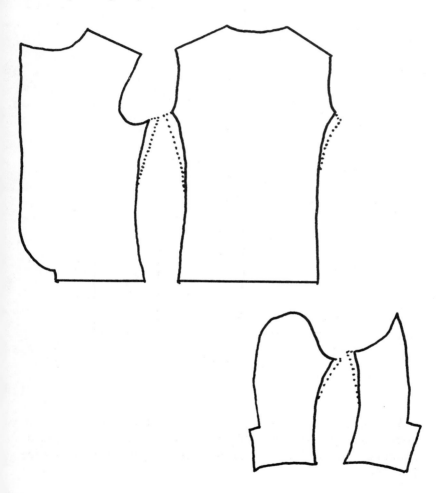

Figure 73

This is a simple alteration, yet too often we are inclined to scoop out the armhole, which only makes things worse—for we have taken fabric away from an area that actually needs more.

If the man is tall and needs extra length in the jacket, the easiest way to alter is simply to slash the pattern in half and drop it down, adding length as necessary. Do the reverse to shorten (See Fig. 74).

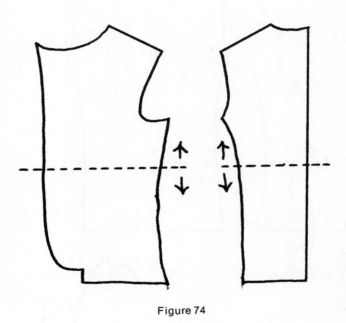

Figure 74

If you have a problem with the back of the jacket pulling up and not hanging straight, this means he is probably stooped or rounded. You will have to allow more length in the back (See Fig. 75).

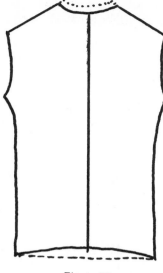

Figure 75

If the collar stands away from the neckline, undoubtedly it is too large and will have to be made smaller. This alteration is generally made in the shoulder seams and in the collar itself (See Fig. 76).

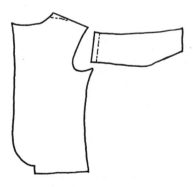

Figure 76

The reverse is true of a collar that hugs the neckline too snugly. Adjust in the shoulder areas and increase the back of the collar (See Fig. 77).

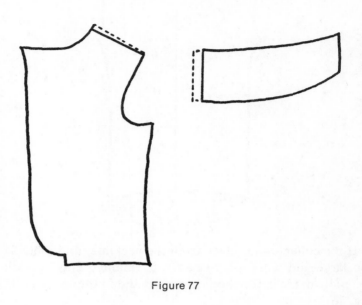

Figure 77

If the shoulders are too erect, you may have to take off some of the back shoulder and cut the front shoulder higher. This usually requires an alteration in the back neck because the shoulders are high in relation to the neck (See Fig. 78).

For a short neck you will also have to lower the neckline. The collar will have to be adjusted accordingly (See Fig. 79).

Very often, a peculiar wrinkle appears below the center back neck, between the shoulders. To alter, you merely scoop out the back neck edge. This will lower the collar and alleviate the fullness (See Fig. 80).

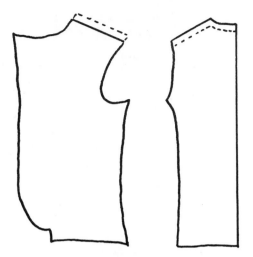

Figure 78

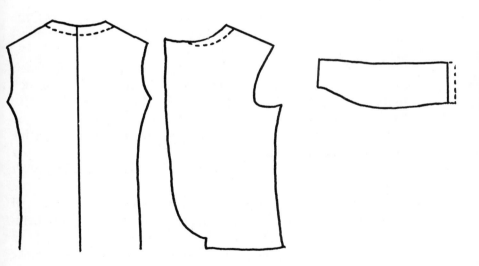

Figure 79

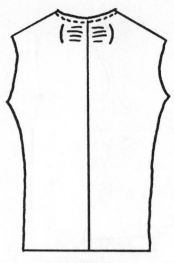

Figure 80

For a man with narrow shoulders, you must trim off the edges of the shoulders on the front and back pattern; but don't forget to also add to the top of the sleeves (See Fig. 81).

If the jacket fits fine every other place but the front lapels droop, you will have to raise the lapels. Merely take a slight tuck in the front neck edge in order to shorten this area (See Fig. 82). The collar will not need alteration with this change.

If you need ease around the body, add to the seams in the front and back (See Fig. 83).

To take in body fabric, do the reverse, also taking in deeper front darts if necessary.

Be sure to transfer any and all alterations to every piece of your pattern involved in the change. The main thing to remember in pattern alterations is to use common sense.

After looking over your pattern, you may decide to make some design changes, such as lapel width or pocket shape.

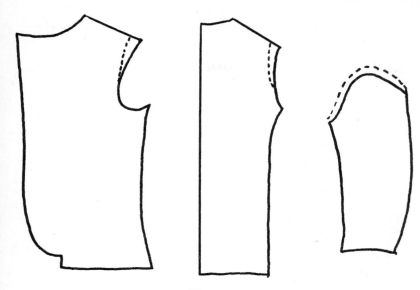

Figure 81

Figure 82

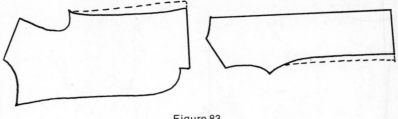

Figure 83

Most of the designing of *lapels* consists of cutting off or adding on to the lapel area. It's a very easy change to make on the front edge of the lapel (See Fig. 84).

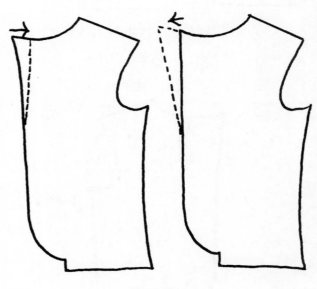

Figure 84

The notch can be moved backward or forward to make a shorter or longer gorgeline (See Fig. 85).

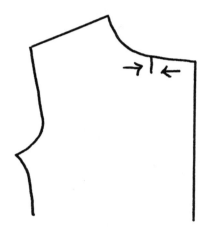

Figure 85

The collar will have to be changed accordingly. The only parts of the collar to be changed will be the outer edges and length (See Fig. 86).

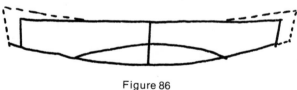

Figure 86

Do not change the neckline edge, as that would alter your neck measurement.

Pockets are fun to change around to suit personal taste. You can change the shape of flaps to your own desire. Here are some suggestions in Figure 87.

Patch pockets can also be changed (See Fig. 88).

Take your pick and have fun custom-designing the jacket!

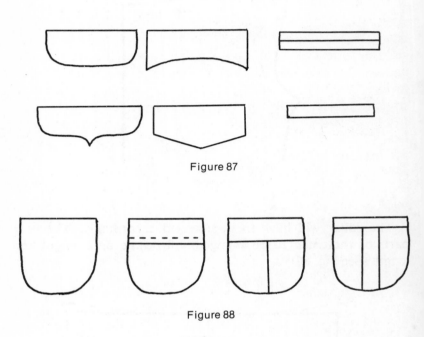

Figure 87

Figure 88

INNER FABRICS

Every professionally sewn jacket depends on its inner fabrics for shape and stability. A good choice of interfacing, lining, and interlining not only considers function but considers the combination of fabrics that work together in each garment.

CHOOSING INNER SHAPING

The best way to decide which interfacing to use is to place your garment fabric over the inner fabric and see how they combine. Drape them over your hand and see how they react together. Be sure the inner fabric doesn't change or overpower the natural characteristics of the garment fabric. However, interfacing must be firm enough to give support and to stabilize a stretchy fabric. Fusible interfacings have added stiffness after fusing, so you should iron on a sample before deciding whether or not to use one.

There are packages available for menswear with ready-made chest pieces, interfacings, shoulder pads, sleeve heads, and other jacket findings. These packages eliminate some of the work in a jacket, but they do add considerable expense. You can make or buy all of the ingredients found in these packages separately.

Interfacing is the layer of fabric placed between garment fabric and the facing or lining to add body and shape, give support, prevent stretching, and define the design lines. You may find that two or even three different fabrics are needed for one garment. A jacket, for example, may have hair canvas interfacing the fronts, lapels, chest piece, and collar; a lightweight canvas for the hems; and muslin for the upper back.

Lining is the inner layer of fabric that is attached with its wrong side against the wrong side of the garment. It finishes the inside of the garment, protects the garment from changes in shape during wearing, and helps reduce wrinkling. In a man's jacket a lining may be partial or complete.

Interlining is a layer of fabric attached to the wrong side of the garment fabric to give extra warmth to the jacket. It also helps to hold a loosely woven fabric in shape.

TYPES OF INTERFACING

There are three groups of interfacings: wovens, non-wovens, and fusibles. By their nature each group requires different handling. Wovens and non-wovens need to be sewn in place, while a fusible is bonded using heat, moisture, and firm pressure.

Woven interfacings are usually cut on the same grain as the piece they support. One exception is the interfaced hem, which uses bias strips of interfacing. All woven inner fabrics should be preshrunk in the same manner as the outer fabric.

Hair canvas has a percentage of wool and/or goat hair in it which makes it resilient and especially suited to shaping a tailored garment.

Non-woven interfacings do not have a grain line. This makes it possible to cut the pattern pieces in any direction. All bias non-wovens are suitable to many fabrics for body and shape retention. Very stiff non-wovens are suitable only for waistbands where no stretch is involved.

Fusible interfacings may be woven or non-woven. The fusing agent on one side of the fabric melts when heat, steam, and pressure are applied, and the interfacing is permanently bonded to the back of your garment fabric. A regular interfacing may be fused to small areas with fusing web. Before applying fusible interfacing to the fabric, ½ inch (1.2 cm) is trimmed from seam allowances, leaving ⅛ inch (3 mm) to be caught into the seam. Most fusibles require plenty of steam (using a damp press cloth) and a minimum of 10 seconds of pressure; but always follow specific product instructions carefully.

CUTTING INSTRUCTIONS

With a man's jacket it is easy to become overwhelmed with all those pattern pieces in the beginning. I suggest that you simply cut what is necessary in the beginning and cut the rest as needed. That way you have fewer pieces to worry about and fewer to get mislaid. Initially, you need to cut out the jacket fronts, back, facings, and sleeves. But it is important to lay out all necessary pieces before cutting, to make sure you have enough fabric for your layout.

In cutting *plaids,* you need to match the design at side seams, front facings, center back, and upper and lower sleeve seams. The only place you will be able to match the sleeves to the jacket will be from mid-front to shoulder seam. The back sleeve seams usually will not match. Just be sure the design runs correctly across the front and into the sleeve. When cutting, match the dots on your upper sleeve seam with the dots on the front armseye.

Cut the lining out completely so you will know how much you have left to use in finishing the jacket, such as pocket facings and guards. The lining should be cut with generous seams. I always suggest adding ⅛ inch (3 mm) to seams to be safe. The lining becomes absorbed and taken up in the jacket, and you will be on the safe side by having a little excess to play with. Also, on sleeves, add ¾ inch (1.8 cm) to top curved sections in order to allow for shoulder padding. This will help keep your lining from pulling (See Fig. 89).

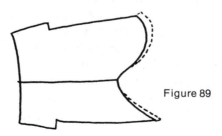

Figure 89

MARKING

After you have cut all the pieces you need, mark all construction symbols. Don't forget to include the dots for sleeve easing, as this insures a correct drape and simplifies adjusting the ease. Roll line, buttonhole placement, center fronts, and slash for notch in lapel can be marked on your front interfacing pieces with a tracing wheel and carbon paper. Snips in the seam line (*small* snips) can be used to indicate markings that fall on the seam line, such as dots in the sleeve seam. Tailor's tacks can also be used; but make sure you use a contrasting thread to enable easy removal after sewing.

I always keep all the pieces and notions for a tailored garment together in a large dress box or something similar. Many of my students use a small suitcase to keep all parts from getting lost, and to make sure they have everything they need when working on their garment.

TRADITIONAL METHOD

Traditional tailoring is a craft which produces a very structured and molded jacket. A well-tailored jacket has sharp, crisp edges and a smooth fit. The collar stand is firm and the lapels hug the jacket. All pockets, flaps, and other details are perfectly stitched. The following techniques are more detailed than those you'll find in your pattern guide. You should follow these instructions to give an expensive, ready-made look to your jacket, but you may occasionally want to refer to your pattern directions for specific detail areas. The techniques that I will be describing are adapted from true tailor's methods using materials available to the home tailor. For the short cut method of tailoring, refer to the Contemporary Method section, which explains the use of fusible interfacing techniques.

Briefly, I will list the things you will need. Have everything you'll need purchased and prepared ahead of time so you won't need to stop in the middle of a sewing session. In addition to fabric, interfacing, and lining, you'll need ¼ inch (6 mm) twill tape to use wherever tape is indicated. Preshrink the tape by dipping the entire card into hot water, bend the card in half to allow for shrinkage, and then let dry on the card. Shoulder pads, chest pads, and sleeve heads may be purchased or made following instructions in this section. You will need about ½ yard (45.8 cm) of unbleached muslin to use for the back interfacing. Wash this in sudsy water and rinse thoroughly to remove all sizing. You will also need approximately 1½ yards of hair canvas for 2 chest pieces and ¼ yard of lamb's wool or high loft polyester fleece for 2 sleeve heads. Buy pocket lining for use inside all the pockets, or else use a firmly woven fabric such as broadcloth. Double strands of your regular thread may be used for topstitching, or you may use buttonhole twist if you prefer. Don't forget to buy buttons in two sizes; larger ones for the front opening and smaller ones for the sleeves.

FRONT UNIT PREPARATION

If you have cut everything out according to directions, you are ready to stitch in the front darts. One tip: Be sure, at the tapered end of each dart, that you sew 3 or 4 stitches barely on the fabric to guarantee a smooth dart. This will eliminate the homemade pucker. Before pressing, a tiny snip in the middle of the dart should be sufficient to turn the dart toward center fronts.

The next step is a simple but important one. You are going to shape (shrink out) the hollow of the front shoulder area. This will give you slightly contoured shoulders when you join the shoulder seams. Some fabrics will shrink more readily and shape more easily than others.

Here's how it's done: On the *wrong* side of your garment, ease the fabric with your left hand, putting your steam iron down with your right. Don't steam in wrinkles; just ease the fabric in (See Fig. 90).

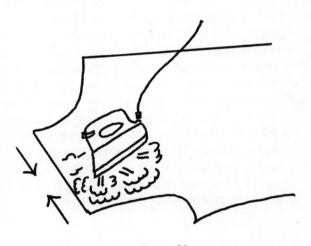

Figure 90

To prepare the fronts for the pockets, mark the ends of the pocket mouthlines on the right side of the fabric with chalk. On the *wrong* side, pin a 2" x 9" (5 cm x 22.9 cm) piece of muslin or similar fabric over each pocket mouthline for stability. Then you ignore this stay and treat it as one piece of fabric. If you have a two-piece front, you will need to join the two pieces before attaching this stay.

POCKETS

Pocket making is probably the most frightening aspect of your jacket project because you have to slash into that beautiful piece of fabric—and it's right in the front, too! However, if you become familiar with what you are doing before working on your jacket, you'll see that pockets are actually much easier than you imagined.

Make lower front pockets now. The upper pocket is made now if it's a patch pocket, but if it's a welt pocket, wait until the interfacing is in place.

I will discuss and describe several methods for making pockets so that you can decide which is most suitable for your jacket. Always make a sample out of scraps of your fabric or muslin so that you know exactly what you're working toward.

PATCH POCKETS

In men's jackets I prefer the machine-sewn pocket for stability and ease of insertion. This pocket is completely sewn in by machine with no stitches visible on the right side. Topstitching may be added afterwards. The inside is neatly finished with a complete lining enclosing all seams. The lining itself, slightly shorter than the outside pocket, supports the contents of the pocket to prevent distortion. As described, the method is for patch pockets with rounded edges, but it can also be done with a square pocket by making a couple of changes. I will discuss these changes after showing you the basic steps.

1. Marking: Mark the placement of the pocket on jacket with hand-basting. Mark fold line on the pocket.

2. Joining lining: Cut 2 lining sections the same size as the *finished* pocket. With top edges even and right sides together, center one lining section on pocket. Stitch a ⅝ inch (1.5 cm) seam at top edge, leaving ½ inch (1.2 cm) free at each end (See Fig. 91). Press lining up

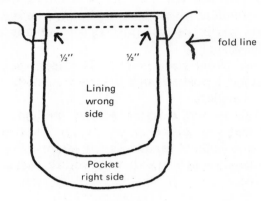

½"   ½"

fold line

Lining
wrong
side

Pocket
right side

Figure 91

3. On other lining section, press top edge ¼ inch (6 mm) to wrong side. Pin lining sections right side together, matching curved bottom edges. Stitch ⅝ inch (1.5 cm) seam around cut edge. Trim lining seam allowance to ¼ inch (6 mm) (See Fig. 92).

4. Folding under edges: Turn top edge of pocket to inside along marked fold line; press. Stitch *with contrasting colored thread* around cut edge of pocket ½ inch (1.2 cm) from edge (See Fig. 21).

5. At each curve of pocket, make a line of ease-stitching (longest basting stitch) ¼ inch (6 mm) from cut edge. Fold entire seam allowance under so machine-stitching is rolled ⅛ inch (3 mm) to the wrong side; hand-baste close to fold (See Fig. 93). At curves, pull up basting thread to ease in fullness. With lining under seam allowance, press folded edge lightly.

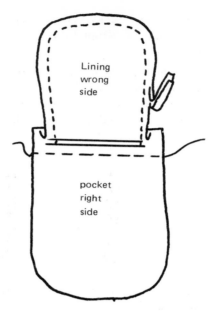

Lining
wrong
side

pocket
right
side

Figure 92

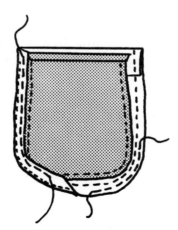

Figure 93

6. Stitching pocket to jacket: Pin pocket on jacket, just inside pocket marking. Set machine for longest, narrowest zigzag stitch and machine-baste pocket to jacket. Zigzag stitches should just catch the edge of the pocket (See Fig. 94). If you don't have a zigzag machine, hand-baste pocket to jacket, using a narrow catch-stitch. Remove the hand-baste pocket to jacket, using a narrow catch-stitch. Remove the hand-basting done in Step 5.

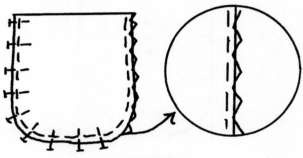

Figure 94

7. On *inside* of pocket, straight-stitch around entire pocket, just inside the row of contrasting stitching (See Fig. 95). (Yes, you really can get the pressure foot in here.) Remove zigzag basting. If curves of pocket are bulky, clip seam allowance.

inside stitching

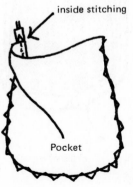

Pocket

Figure 95

8. Finishing: Trim off corners of seam allowances at top of pocket. Without distorting pocket, pin loose edge of pocket lining to jacket. Topstitch in place. At corners, work diagonal bar-tacks long enough to catch in pocket lining (See Fig. 96).

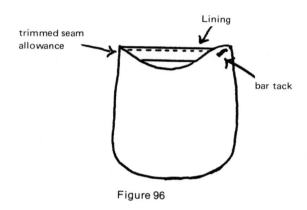

Figure 96

FLAP POCKETS

For each pocket, cut out the following:

1 flap of garment fabric

If plaid or stripe, be sure the fabric design matches where pockets are to be placed.

1 flap of lining material

Self fabric can be substituted for a firmer flap.

2 pieces of pocket material

Cut 7" x 8" (17.8 cm x 20.3 cm) on the straight. If the pocket is put in on a slant, the grain will run the same as the jacket.

1 piece of garment material for welts

Cut 6" x 8" (15.2 cm x 20.3 cm) the same grain as the jacket.

It is rarely necessary to interface the flaps. Stitch your flaps and lining together, right sides together. Take great care to make sure the flaps are stitched evenly. To get good corners on your flaps, always use small stitches and sew two stitches diagonally across the points. The diagonal stitching absorbs the excess fullness at the points and you end up with sharp, smooth, professional corners. Use this method anywhere in the jacket where a good point is desired (See Fig. 97).

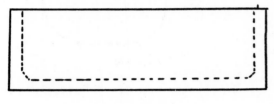

Figure 97

After the flaps are stitched, trim closely, especially the corners; grade seams, turn, and press. If you want to topstitch the flaps, do so now.

Now, stitch one piece of pocket material to each side of the welt piece in ½ inch (1.2 cm) seams (See Fig. 98). Press the seams toward the pocket material. Slash welt piece in half.

You are now ready to assemble the pocket. Pin the raw edge of each flap to the upper edge of each mouthline, right sides together (See Fig. 99).

You will have to baste if you are matching plaids or stripes in order to avoid slippage. With the right sides together, place one welt piece over each flap along the upper edge of the mouthline

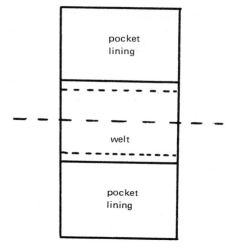

Figure 98

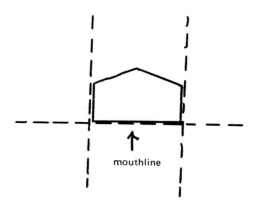

Figure 99

(See Fig. 100). Then line up the remaining welt piece to the bottom of the mouthline, butting it up against the edges of the flap and top welt (See Fig. 101).

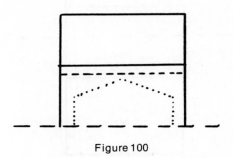

Figure 100

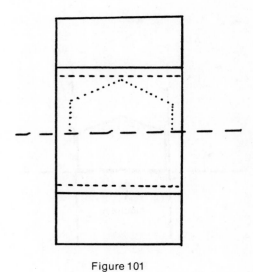

Figure 101

Now, stitch approximately ¼ inch (6 mm) on each side of this mouthline, stopping and starting where you have chalk-marked on the ends of the pocket. The upper line of stitching should begin and end precisely at the edges of the finished flap and the lower line should be approximately 2 stitches less on each end, so that the flap will cover the welt when finished (See Fig. 102).

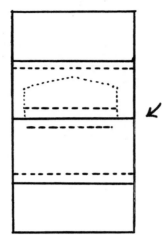

Figure 102

Also be sure to lock your stitches on each end of all stitching lines so that they will not fray out when you clip the corners.

Turn garment to the wrong side. The size of this rectangle will determine the size of the lower welt you will make. Slash between the two stitchings, cutting outward to the corners (See Fig. 103).

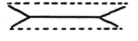

Figure 103

Give yourself at least ½ inch (1.2 cm) corners to handle. And also be sure that you clip into the very end stitches of the corners to make a neat turn. Pull all the material through the opening to the wrong side. Press the upper pocket piece down. Press top pocket seam upward (See Fig. 104). Lift both sections of the pocket up and press the bottom seam upward (See Fig. 105).

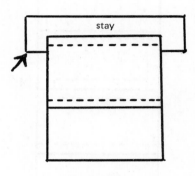

Figure 104

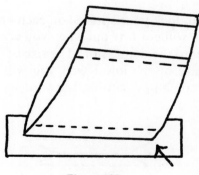

Figure 105

Fold both pocket pieces back down and turn the jacket to the right side. Lift up the flap and pull the bottom welt piece up, filling the entire opening. Straighten the little fold (which is actually an extension of the welt) on each side underneath the opening and make an even welt. Press this welt in place and pin to anchor it. Then, lift the garment and stay back, and stitch the corners of each side of the welts, anchoring them with stitching (sew back and forth several times) (See Fig. 106).

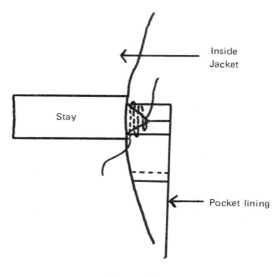

Inside
Jacket

Stay

Pocket lining

Figure 106

You can topstitch this welt in place on the right side through the previously stitched seam line, sometimes called "stitching in the ditch." Fold the flap back down and stitch ⅛ inch (3 mm) above the flap seamline through all thicknesses (See Fig. 107).

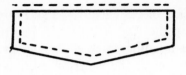

Figure 107

Now you're ready to give your finished pocket a good pressing. Place a damp pressing cloth over the top of each flap. Then press with your iron, lift your press cloth, and give it a good whack with your pounder. This will flatten your flaps and give them that good professional look.

To close up your finished pockets, just stitch the edges in a regular seam allowance and zigzag to finish the raw edges.

DOUBLE WELT POCKET WITH FLAP

This pocket is similar to a "windowpane" bound buttonhole. The flap is inserted between the two ¼ inch (6 mm) wide welts, so that the finished jacket can be worn with the flap inside or outside the pocket. The length of the windowpane is determined by your pattern; the width of the windowpane must be ½ inch (1.2 cm).

1. Cutting: For each pocket, cut the following—using your patterns:

Upper Flap—out of your garment fabric
Under Flap—out of your lining fabric, or use garment
        fabric for firmer flap
Pocket—out of pocket lining fabric
Underlay—out of jacket lining fabric, the width of the
        pocket pattern and 3 inches (7.6 cm) long

Two welts—out of garment fabric, each the width of
pocket pattern and 2 inches (5 cm) long.

2. Preparing pocket: Mark windowpane on *wrong* side of
pocket, following your pattern. On underlay, turn and press
one long edge ¼ inch (6 mm) to the wrong side. On opposite
end, place the wrong side of the underlay on the right side of
the pocket, matching raw edges; stitch in place (See Fig. 108).

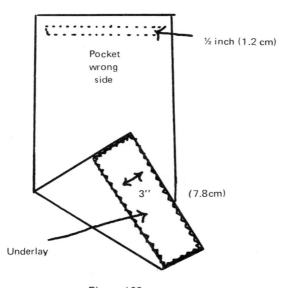

Figure 108

3. Making windowpane: Pin right side of pocket to right side
of jacket, matching windowpanes. Using 12-15 stitches per inch
and beginning at the center of one long side, stitch very accurately around marked windowpane.

4. Slash carefully through center of windowpane, stopping ½ inch (1.2 cm) from ends; clip diagonally into each corner, forming triangles at ends (See Fig. 109). Turn pocket to wrong side of jacket; press.

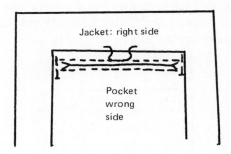

Figure 109

5. Putting in the welts: Place welts right sides together and machine-baste down center; fold each welt so stitching is inside and press. To stabilize welts, fuse a strip of something like Magic Polyweb or Stitch Witchery inside the folded edges (see Fig. 110).

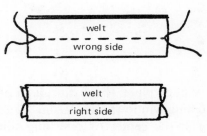

Figure 110

6. Working from the right side of jacket, center welts under windowpane, making sure that each welt is exactly ¼ inch (6 mm) wide; pin. Be sure welts extend beyond both ends of opening. Set machine at longest, narrowest, zigzag stitch. On the two long edges, zigzag-baste welts to jacket with stitches, barely catching the edge of the windowpane (See Fig. 111). If you don't have a zigzag machine, slipstitch in place by hand.

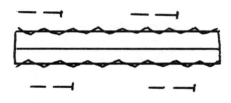

Figure 111

7. To stitch *bottom* welt in place, fold jacket so bottom seam allowance of windowpane is exposed. Using stitching line of windowpane as a guide, baste through seam allowances of windowpane and welt. If welt is straight and even, stitch exactly over basting with regular machine-stitches; back-tack (See Fig. 112).

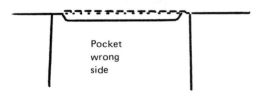

Pocket
wrong
side

Figure 112

8. To stitch *top* welt permanently in place, fold jacket so top seam allowance of windowpane is exposed. Stitch the same as you did the bottom welt.

9. Stitch sides of welts in the same manner; carefully sew back and forth several times to secure triangles.

10. Zigzag over raw edges of welts, catching them to pocket only (See Fig. 113). Remove zigzag-basting along welts; remove basting holding welts together.

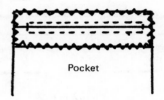

Pocket

Figure 113

11. Flap: For the flap to roll slightly to the underside, trim ⅛ inch (3 mm) off sides and bottom of under flap. With raw edges matching, join upper and under flaps, leaving top edge open. Trim and grade seam allowance; turn and press. Baste top edges of flap together, ⅝ inch (1.5 cm) from raw edge.

12. Slip flap under top welt, lining up basting stitches on flap with upper part of top welt; pin. "Stitch in the ditch" through welt and flap (See Fig. 114).

Figure 114

13. Forming the pocket: Fold pocket up; right sides together, raw edges even; stitch side seams, rounding off bottom corners. Stitch again ⅛ inch (3 mm) away.

14. To hold top seam allowance of pocket in upward position, fold jacket to expose top edge of pocket. Stitch across top of pocket, through all layers, ⅛ inch (3 mm) away from previous stitching.

BREAST POCKET ON LEFT FRONT

You may place a welt pocket, flap pocket, or a patch pocket in this area. The flap pocket and patch pocket will be exactly like the previous directions, with smaller measurements.

For the flap pocket or welt pocket, cut pocket material 6½ inches (16.5 cm) deep and 2 inches (5 cm) longer than the mouthline.

WELT POCKET

First, determine the length of the welt from the pattern. The welt is generally made out of two pieces of self-fabric and finished on three sides before being basted to the *lower* mouthline, raw side up (See Fig. 115).

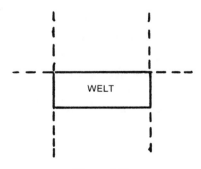

Figure 115

Then, using the same method you used in making the lower pockets, you will stitch and slash. The welt is then brought up and tacked in place by hand.

INTERFACING JACKET FRONTS

To give additional support to the jacket front, extend the front interfacing to the underarm seam from below the armhole and to the dart. Using your jacket front pattern and your interfacing patterns, draw a new cutting line starting 3 inches (7.6 cm) below the armhole seam line and curving into the end of dart, following dart on center foldline (See Fig. 116).

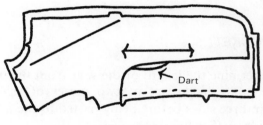

Figure 116

Cut interfacing from hair canvas and mark roll line with tracing wheel and dressmaker's carbon. Also mark center front lines and buttonhole placement at this time.

Pin interfacing to wrong side of fabric along all edges, being sure that lapel and upper shoulder areas are carefully matched. There may be slight inaccuracies due to irregularities in cutting, so do not force edges together. Remember that interfacing should work with and shape the outer fabric, not distort its intended shape.

Hand-baste the roll line in place with a long running stitch through both thicknesses. To prevent shifting during construction, tailor-baste the interfacing in place below the roll line to within 1 inch (2.5 cm) from edges. Leave lapel edges free until you pad-stitch (See Fig. 117).

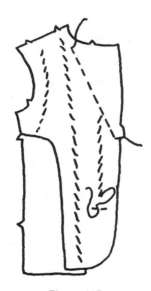

Figure 117

If slash pockets have been put in jacket, cut out a small piece of canvas at top of each pocket and pull the pockets out over the canvas. Catch-stitch in place along the fronts and tops of the pockets as far as possible. This will keep the pockets in position (See Fig. 118).

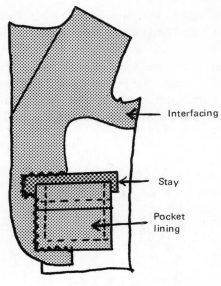

Interfacing

Stay

Pocket lining

Figure 118

Trim ¾ inch (1.8 cm) from interfacing edges along side seam, shoulder, neck, and front edges. (Leave full seam in armhole edge.) This will keep the hair canvas out of your seam allowance and help you get sharper edges when pressing. Machine-baste armhole edge ½ inch (1.2 cm) from edge.

TAPING AND PAD STITCHING

You are now ready to tape the fronts. This is the professional way to put a jacket together with those fine, smooth edges. Although it requires a great deal of patience and handwork, you will be rewarded when you see how simply it goes together. And wait till you see the finished product! If you run your thread through some beeswax, you will have less problems of thread knotting with all your handwork. I usually like to do this part while relaxing and enjoying television, as it does take time.

Using either ⅜ inch (9 mm) or ¼ inch (6 mm) twill tape, start 2 inches (5 cm) above the buttonhole area on the canvas and end an inch before the neck seam. Cut tape ½ inch (1.2 cm) shorter than this measurement. Place tape *behind* the marked roll line of both canvas fronts. The tape should be pulled slightly as you apply it in order to control the bias and keep the lapels flat on the chest. Anchor the tape with small running stitches. Try to catch only the canvas and tape. Since you could accidentally catch the outer fabric, make sure you are using matching thread. And use the same amount of tape for both canvases, so that your fronts will be identical.

Now catch-stitch each side of the tape to the canvas with ½ inch (1.2 cm) stitches (See Fig. 119).

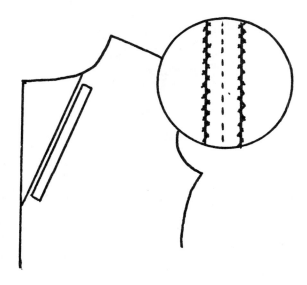

Figure 119

Pad-stitch the lapels to create permanent shaping and insure that it will last. This is done with matching thread. Place the lapel over your hand in the position it will be worn. Rows of pad-stitching are parallel to the roll line and about ¼ inch (6 mm) apart. Stitches should be about ½ inch (1.2 cm) in length. Start the first row next to the roll line and work back and forth, always keeping the lapel in the same position. When near the point of the lapel, make your stitches shorter and the rows closer together to make the point firmer. This helps keep the finished lapel point flat on the body (See Fig. 120).

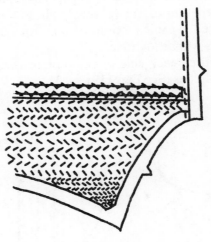

Figure 120

You must remember not to pull your pad-stitches tightly. when the lapel area is completely padded, you will have a definite roll to the lapel, but no pulling anywhere.

From now on, be sure you work from the neck edge down on the right front, and from the bottom up on the left front. If you keep this in mind, you will find that your stitches will always be going in the correct direction and you will be assembling properly.

Pin the ¼ inch (6 mm) tape all along the front edges, slightly over the trimmed canvas. Start from the neck edge of the roll line tape and continue down the entire front. Be sure that tape is eased around the corner of the lapel. (The tape is just twisted at the corner). Pull a little tighter in the center of the lapel area, ease around the buttonhole area, and pull a little tighter again in the curved area of the hip (See Fig. 121). The shoulder seam tape should just meet, not overlap, the neckline tape.

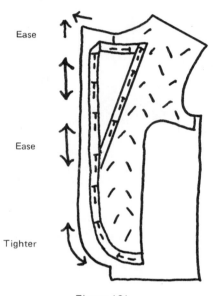

Figure 121

If your jacket does not have a front curve, simply carry the tape down, twisting at the corner as in the lapel area, and stop at the end of the canvas.

You are controlling the shaping of the jacket with this taping. Attach the inner edge of the tape with small running stitches to the interfacing only. Catch-stitch the outer edge of the seam allowance of the garment with stitches about ½ inch (1.2 cm) in length. These stitches must not be tight as they'll eventually be caught into the seam when you join the facing to the jacket (See Fig. 122).

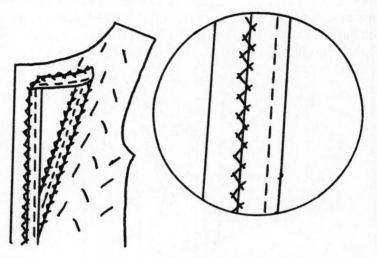

Figure 122

After both sides are taped, lightly press the lapels and front areas. You should now have neat, taped fronts with controlled shaping and no pulling.

CHEST PIECE

The chest piece rounds out the natural hollow in front of the man's shoulder. Use your interfacing pattern piece as a guide, drawing in three different shapes as shown in Figure 123.

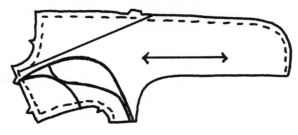

Figure 123

Each chest piece is constructed with four layers of hair canvas in graduated shapes—2 chest piece layers, 1 armhole reinforcement, and 1 shoulder pad pocket (See Fig. 124).

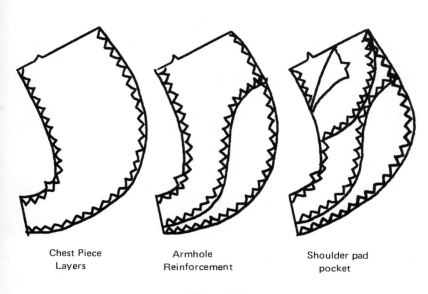

| Chest Piece | Armhole | Shoulder pad |
| Layers | Reinforcement | pocket |

Figure 124

The bottom *chest piece layers* extend from the armhole and shoulder to 2½ inches (6.4 cm) below the armhole seam. They do not curve into the neck seam; they end ½ inch (1.2 cm) from the roll line.

The *armhole reinforcement* is the same as the chest piece except that the inside edge curves from 4 inches (10.2 cm) below the shoulder to 2 inches (5 cm) below the armhole, as illustrated.

The *shoulder pad pocket* is 6 inches (15.2 cm) wide along the shoulder and 6 inches (15.2 cm) deep along the armhole, curving as shown.

Transfer each shape onto hair canvas using dressmaker's carbon. For two chest pieces, cut out 4 chest piece layers, 2 armhole reinforcement layers, and 2 shoulder pad pockets. The two bottom chest piece layers may be fused together using a fusible web, or they may be zigzagged together. When using the zigzag method, use longest, widest stitch. Stitch along inside curved edge of the chest pieces and along the armhole edge, leaving opening at the shoulder and armhole where the shoulder pad will be inserted.

Reverse the diagrams in Fig. 124 when constructing the chest piece for the other side of the jacket.

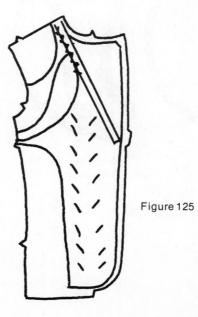

Figure 125

Place chest piece to jacket front so largest layer is next to the front interfacing; the smallest layer will be next to the body. Pin in place with armhole and shoulder edges even. Tailor-baste lightly to keep it from shifting. Catch-stitch the edge next to the roll line, attaching chest piece to interfacing only (See Fig. 125).

JACKET BACKS

Join the backs of the jacket together. Press open. Press the vents according to your pattern instructions.

When completely lining the jacket, I recommend interfacing the upper back with muslin or other lightweight woven interfacing to give extra strength and stability.

Use your back pattern piece as a guide for cutting the muslin, curving the bottom edge from a point about 10 inches (25.4 cm) from the neck edge at center back to a point 3 inches (7.6 cm) below armhole seam. Cut interfacing on the straight grain. Join muslin at center back by overlapping seam lines; zigzag together. Trim seams close to stitching.

To attach interfacing, pin to wrong side of back and machine baste ½ inch (1.2 cm) from edge along sides, armholes, shoulders, and neck. Trim close to stitching.

Stay the neckline edge of the back by stitching in a piece of narrow tape ½ inch (1.2 cm) from back neck edge (See Fig. 126). This will prevent the neck edge from stretching out of shape as you continue working on the jacket.

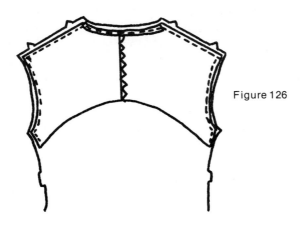

Figure 126

UNDERARM INTERFACING

Cut interfacing for underarm sections using underarm pattern piece as a guide. Interfacing should extend from armhole cutting line to 3 inches (7.6 cm) below the seam line. Trim seam allowances from side seams. Machine-baste to armhole edge ½ inch (1.2 cm) from edge. Catch-stitch in place along side seams (See Fig. 127).

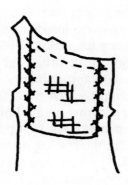

Figure 127

HEM AND VENT INTERFACING

For hem interfacing, cut bias stripe of hair canvas 1½ inches (3.8 cm) wide; cut 2 strips the measurement of lower edge of jacket fronts and underarm sections. For jacket backs, cut 1 strip the measurement of lower edge and the other 2 inches (5 cm) shorter. Cut vent interfacing 2 inches (5 cm) wide and the length of the vent. Place vent interfacing along the inside of the foldline. Always interface the vent layer that will be toward the garment's outside. Place hem interfacing strips exactly on the hemline, reaching from inside the seam lines to vent interfacing on left back and to vent foldline on right back. Catch-stitch all edges in place (See Fig. 128).

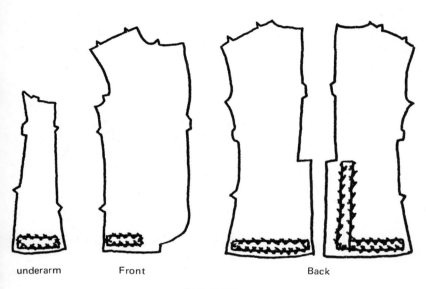

underarm   Front   Back

Figure 128

Sew the sides of the jacket together. Pulling the chest pads away from the seam areas of the front, sew the shoulder seams together, easing the back onto the shaped front shoulder seams. Don't trim the padding.

This is a good time to try the jacket on. You can make minor adjustments and check your progress without too much difficulty. When you are happy with the fit, give the seams a good press.

SLEEVES

Stay-stitch the armhole edge ½ inch (1.2 cm) from the edge for a guide to attach the tape, pulling the chest pad temporarily out of the way. Place and stitch ¼ inch (6 mm) twill tape along this stay-stitching, so that it lies outside the seam allowance, and so that *none* will be caught in the ⅝ inch (1.5 cm) seam (See Fig. 129).

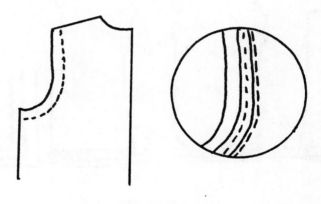

Figure 129

Sew the underarm seams of the sleeves. Press open, using a sleeve board or seam roll. Follow your pattern directions for finishing the hem and vent at lower edge of sleeve—if you are certain of sleeve measurements. If not, wait until sleeves are inserted into garment before you finish the lower edge of the sleeve.

To ease in the top of sleeve, machine-baste between notches, directly on the ⅝ inch (1.5 cm) seam line. Pull up gently to shape, and pin in each sleeve by the markings. Make sure that the chest pads are pulled completely away from the sleeve area and anchored temporarily with a pin. Stitch the sleeve into the jacket directly on top of the previous machine-stitching which has created a well in which to do this stitching—thus eliminating any ripples or puckers. You will be stitching with the sleeve facing you (See Fig. 130).

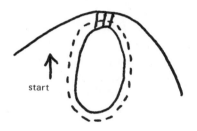

Figure 130

Start the stitching ahead of the underarm marking so that you will go up and around the shoulder, and down around the underarm, and end on the bias. By stitching in this direction you will have less tendency to pull your fabric off grain—and the material will ease in smoothly.

After the first stitching, check the jacket and sleeve to make sure nothing is caught. Put another row of stitching right next to the first stitching, and your sleeve is set in.

Trim seam allowances *below* notches to ¼ inch (6 mm), being careful not to cut tape. Press seam *above* notches open over pressing ham, using just the tip of the iron. Trim rest of seam allowances to ⅜ inch (9 mm).

You might check the drape of the sleeves at this point. Put your fist inside each shoulder and make sure the sleeve has a tendency to drape forward over the lower front pockets. You will be able to see the general swing of the sleeves now.

SHOULDER PADS

Put shoulder pads into jacket with approximately ⅓ of the pad in front of the shoulder seam and in the shoulder pad pocket, and ⅔ of the pad in back. The armhole edge of the pad should extend ⅜ inch (9 mm) beyond the seam line.

You are now ready to finish the sleeves professionally. On the *outside* of the shoulder, pull the fabric taut over your fist, in the direction on the top of the sleeve. Be sure the fabric fits smoothly on the top of each shoulder. When you are satisfied, tailor-baste the top of the shoulder with large stitches through all thicknesses, anchoring all padding. Don't be afraid to stick that needle way down inside that padding. Now, run one more row of tailor-basting along the sleeve seam, again through the padding; go through as much as possible (See Fig. 131).

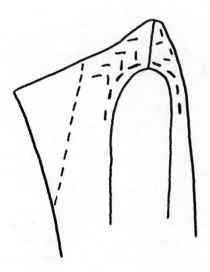

Figure 131

Turn to the inside of the sleeve, open the sleeve seam you previously had pressed open, and lay it flat against the padding so that the padding is actually lying on top of an opened seam. Let the lower armhole fall into a double seam again (See Fig. 132).

Figure 132

Pin the opened seam in place against the padding. Then trim off the excess padding, if any, even with the trimmed seam edge. Now anchor the seam, padding, and canvas together with a strong backstitch and double thread. You now have anchored the entire shoulder, canvas, and padding to the sleeves. Catch-stitch upper edge of shoulder pad pocket to shoulder pad and lower edge of chest piece to side seam.

SLEEVE HEADS

Sleeve heads give the top of the sleeve cap a smoother line and improve the hang of the sleeve. Make your own sleeve heads out of a lofty non-woven or lamb's wool cut on the bias. Cut two pieces 14 inches (35.6 cm) long and 3 inches (7.6 cm) wide. Fold one long edge over 1 inch (2.5 cm) and stitch ⅜ inch (9 mm) from the fold.

Insert the sleeve head on the sleeve side of the seam. The folded edge is lined up with the cut edge of all the padding. The armhole seam will be in between the padding and the sleeve. The widest edge of the sleeve head will rest against the sleeve, and the folded-back narrower edge will face the inside of the garment. Pin one end at seam where underarm and back are joined and extend other end to front of armhole. Turn back the folded edge and slipstitch to the sleeve seam (See Fig. 133).

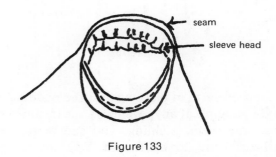

Figure 133

This sleeve method will give you a beautiful professional shoulder which duplicates fine custom-tailoring.

INSIDE POCKETS

Now we start on the inside of the jacket, so the pressure is really off. In here your first time mistakes (if any) won't show!

Sew the front facing to the front lining and stitch in the front dart. If you have a two-piece front lining, stitch the front side piece on at this time. Mark the mouthline for the inside pocket

—it's usually on the right side of the jacket. Sometimes a pattern won't have markings for the inside pocket, so you just measure 1½ inches (3.8 cm) down from the underarm and end about ¾ inch (1.8 cm) into the facing. The pocket mouthline will vary in style, but it would not be any longer than 6 inches (15.2 cm) in finished width (See Fig. 134).

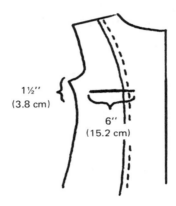

Figure 134

You can simply chalk-mark, on the right side, this mouthline and both ends. For stability, pin a piece of muslin stay underneath the pocket mouthline on the wrong side (See Fig. 135).

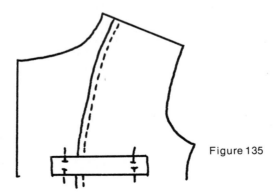

Figure 135

Cut a piece of pocket material 8'' x 16'' (20.3 cm x 40.6 cm), on the straight of grain. This can be cut longer or shorter depending on pocket depth. Face the middle portion of the pocket with a 5'' x 8'' (12.7 cm x 20.3 cm) piece of lining or garment fabric. On knits or heavier fabrics, the lining fabric is more desirable; and on fine woolen or lightweight fabrics, a facing of the garment fabric itself seems to work best. Turn under the raw edges of this facing, and topstitch it to the pocket lining (See Fig. 136).

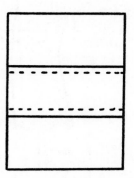

Figure 136

With a tracing wheel, mark the pocket opening on the pocket to use as a stitching guide.

Pin pocket face down to the right side of the lining and facing, matching end markings. Stitch around the four sides of the pocket, using a small stitch (15-20 stitches per inch). Slash all thicknesses through center of stitching to ½ inch (1.2 cm) from ends and clip to outer corners as close to stitching as possible (See Fig. 137).

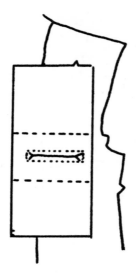

Figure 137

Turn pocket through slash to inside. Press the long slashed edges toward the opening and the slipped V-shaped corners away from the opening.

To form welts, make an inverted box pleat in the opening with pocket fabric. Baste around the opening, keeping welts in place (See Fig. 138).

Topstitch from the right side in the two grooves formed by the welt seams (stitch in the ditch) (See Fig. 139).

From the inside, stitch V-shaped corners, welts, and pocketing together along ends of pocket opening (See Fig. 140).

Pin remaining three sides of pocket together and machine-stitch, again catching in V-shaped corners. Stitch again ¼ inch (6 mm) outside first stitching. Trim seam (See Fig. 67).

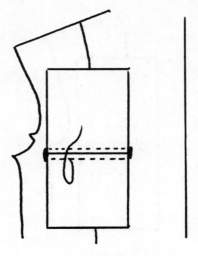

Figure 138

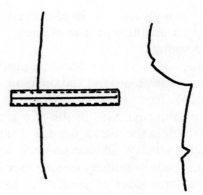

Figure 139

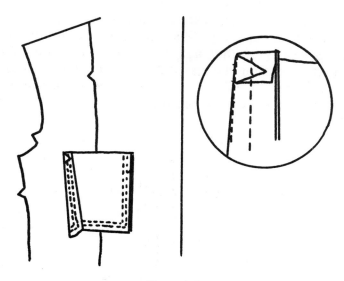

Figure 140

ARMHOLE GUARDS

Most expensive garments have guards under the armholes to prolong the life of the lining. There are various methods of inserting these, and this is how I do it on a fully-lined jacket.

Cut a guard approximately 3½'' x 4½'' (8.8 x 11.4 cm) in a shield shape out of your jacket fabric (See Fig. 141).

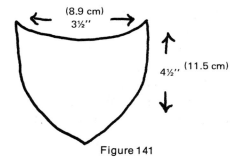

Figure 141

Cut out a 1½" (3.8 cm) wide bias strip of lining material (this can be pieced if necessary). Place the bias strip on top of the guard, right sides together, and stitch in a ¼ inch (6 mm) seam all around, stretching the bias to fit. Fold the bias strip to the inside, over the ¼ inch (6 mm) seam. Press and topstitch through all thicknesses (See Fig. 142).

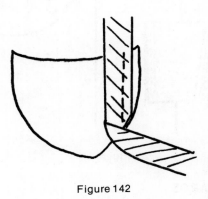

Figure 142

Place the guard in the armhole area of the lining and trim even with the curve of the lower armhole. Topstitch in position and press; then baste remaining raw edges together. The guard will be treated as part of the lining from now on.

FACINGS

All facings on all garments are automatically cut slightly fuller and/or longer in order to allow ease in turning and to allow ease for the seam to roll back and hide on the underside.

Pin front facings to jacket fronts—matching notches and other markings, and easing in the extra fullness on the facings. Stitch on the canvas side only on both sides of the jacket. Put in 1 or 2 stitches diagonally across the corners to give you clean, professional points. Stitch only to the slash mark of the notch. If you find uneven stitching, restitch it now to guarantee a good straight front edge. Now press that seam open. This is where you can get full use out of that point presser. Lay the seam directly on the wooden edge and press open with the tip of your iron. It is much easier to press open a nice wide seam, so press before you trim. After pressing, check the lapel notches to make sure both sides match. Now, trim and grade the entire front seam. The seam edge that lays against the outside of the garment is the one that remains the longest when trimming. Don't forget to reverse your trimming at the roll line.

Turn and press the facing to the inside of the jacket, rolling the seam as you press so that it will not be visible on the outside. Again, reverse the seam in the lapel area so that it will not show when the lapel is turned back. After the seam is in correct position, either by pressing or basting, steam the front edges and use your pounder to set the seam permanently in place. You should have a nice, flat edge when finished.

HEMS

Trim seam allowances below hemline from any seam that extends into the hem allowance (See Fig. 143).

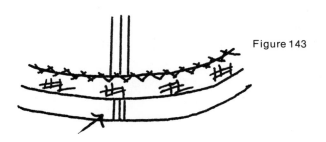

Figure 143

Turn up hem and press. Catch-stitch hems to hem inter-facing. Baste and press vents according to pattern directions. Catch-stitch inner edges of vent and front facing to hem. Lift back the front facing and tack the seam that connects the facing and lining to the canvas underneath, *wherever possible,* in order to keep the front facing in place. Don't tack too closely because you still need to join the shoulders of the lining. Also, catch-stitch the bottom of the inside pockets to the canvas.

LINING

The lining in a man's jacket is very quick and easy to insert. All you do is join the center backs of the lining, and then join at the shoulders and sides. Next, baste the neck edges of the jacket and lining together, and then baste armhole edges together. The results are completely satisfactory and much easier than the custom tailor's hand-sewn method.

Finish off the inside of the jacket before you go on to the collar. Turn under the lining and hem to the jacket, allowing a little ease in order to eliminate pulling at hem edge. Finish off lining to the vents according to your pattern work sheet.

Stitch seams in sleeve lining from armhole to lower edge, omitting the vent. Trim away vent extensions and press seams open. Machine-baste top of sleeve and press under ⅝ inch (1.5 cm) around armhole edge. Turn jacket sleeve and lining sleeve wrong sides out. Match the pressed-open underarm seams, keeping armhole seams even. With long running stitches, sew one seam allowance of the lining to matching seam allowance of the sleeve, starting and ending about 4 inches (10.2 cm) from top and bottom of sleeve (See Fig. 144).

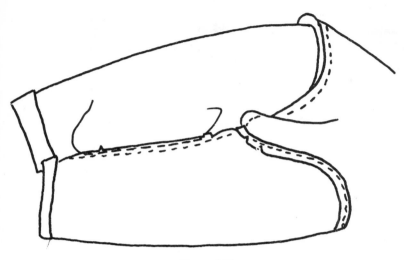

Figure 144

Slip your hand inside the sleeve lining from the armhole. Grasp the lower edge of the jacket sleeve and the lining and pull them both through the lining. The lining is now in place, wrong sides together, and the stitching will keep it from shifting out of place.

Finish off the lining to the vents according to your work sheet. It is easier to sew your sleeve buttons on now before your lining is hemmed to the bottom edge of the sleeve.

Pin and baste sleeve linings to jacket lining, pulling machine-basting stitches to fit. Hem in *small* stitches around the arm-holes. Sometimes I go around twice to make it good and secure (See Fig. 145).

Now examine the jacket closely to make sure there is no pulling anywhere. Put it on him and check again. If there is any pulling, you must open up the jacket and make the necessary adjustments now.

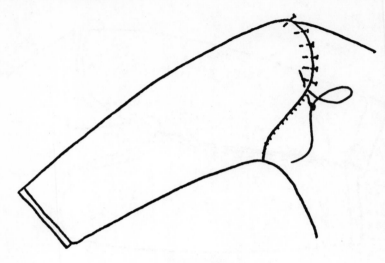

Figure 145

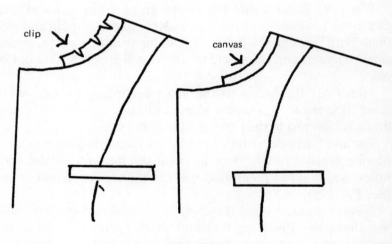

Figure 146

NECKLINE FINISHING

Mark the seam line of the facing gorgeline with chalk. Clip the facing at neck edge to make it lie flat—then turn under as far as the shoulder seam. The shoulder seam can be opened ⅝ inch (1.5 cm) to simplify this (See Fig. 146).

Now baste and press. Invisibly hem the turned-under seam to the canvas, and you have finished off the bottom part of the lapel on the gorgeline. Some interfacing (from the front canvas) will still extend up. This will later be catch-stitched to the canvas of the undercollar.

COLLAR

Most of the work on the collar will be done by hand. Once you understand the principle, you'll find it to be the easiest, smoothest way to put on a collar—a way that shows none of those ugly bulges. You will have a collar that looks, and is, truly professional.

METHOD I (using melton for undercollar)

It is usually impossible to get a perfect match in color, so the undercollar is usually of a blending color when using this method. The undercollar canvas is a stiff interfacing that molds easily and keeps the melton in shape. Both the undercollar and interfacing are cut on the bias. To prepare your pattern for cutting, you must first remove all seam lines, *except center back.* Cut your melton collar out with this pattern, and seam the center back. Press the seam open and trim to ¼ inch (6 mm). Mark the standline and shoulder dots. Lay the undercollar directly over a piece of stiff canvas, seam side down, and machine-stitch directly over the standline (See Fig. 147).

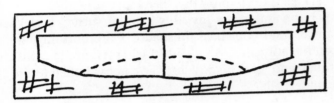

Figure 147

Trim the canvas around the outer shape of the undercollar. Put in two rows of pad-stitching below the standline, starting at one end of the collar and padding parallel with the standline (See Fig. 148).

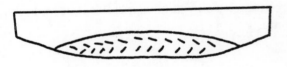

Figure 148

On the other side of the stand line, pad-stitch—again parallel to the standling—and continue until the entire undercollar is padded. This pad-stitching is done on the same principle as the lapel. You may go back and forth, but don't turn the collar. Also, roll the collar over your finger while putting in these stitches.

After padding, trim ⅛ inch (3 mm) away from the canvas completely around the collar to eliminate the canvas from showing. Crease the undercollar on the standline with the melton inside the fold and *hard-press*. Then slightly stretch the outer edges of the collar with your steam iron (See Fig. 149).

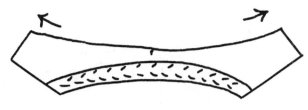

Figure 149

The undercollar will now be slightly curved. Do not pull too much.

Clip back neck edge to stay tape and chalk-mark neckline seam on the outside of the garment. From center back seam, baste the undercollar onto each side, butting up to chalk line, matching shoulder markings and ending the collar at the slashed notch. Hemstitch the collar with fine stitches along the outside seam (See Fig. 150).

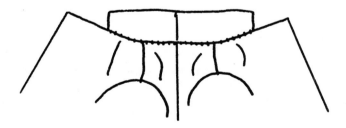

Figure 150

You can now try the jacket on and check roll, length of collar, and general appearance. You can get a clear picture of how it will look when finished.

Catch-stitch the front canvas that is extending up from the jacke to the undercollar canvas. This now anchors everything in the jacket (See Fig. 151).

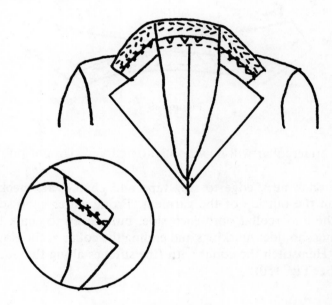

Figure 151

UPPER COLLAR

Cut according to pattern, including any changes you may have made in the undercollar. Stretch the shoulder edges by pulling slightly with your left hand while steaming with the right hand (See Fig. 152).

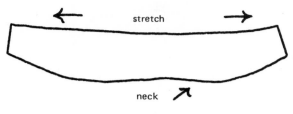

Figure 152

Pin the upper collar onto the undercollar, checking to make sure you have equal amounts of seam all around. Baste directly over the standline, fastening both collars, starting at center back and working to each end. From now until the collar is completely finished, you will be working from center back towards each end. This insures that you have sufficient fabric at both ends to prevent pulling.

Now press the seam edges of the upper collar over the edges of the undercollar. This gives you an accurate guideline to the finished edge. Trim the upper collar seams down to ¼ inch (6 mm). Turn under these seams and place them between the upper collar and the undercollar. Baste the finished edge in place.

Miter the corners of the collar and turn under the neck edge of the collar, butting the fold with the fold of the facing at the gorgeline (See Fig. 153).

Use the felling stitch to attach both upper and undercollars together on the underside. On the gorgeline, invisibly hemstitch the collar to the canvas. Then go back and whip the collar and facing seams together, going from fold to fold of each seam to make sure no canvas shows. Hemstitch the neck edge of the upper collar to the lining, and your collar is completely finished.

Press the lapels and collar, pounding to make them lie flat. Remove any bastings left in the jacket.

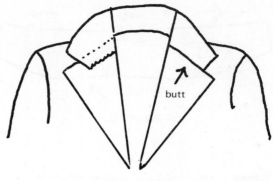

butt

Figure 153

All this handwork is the *easiest* way to get the *flattest* finish and it practically guarantees a professional lapel and collar. It may be fastidious, but the result will make you proud!

METHOD II (Self fabric on undercollar)

This method yields a satisfactory collar, but it will not be as flat as the collar shaping outlined in Method I, because you have extra bulk from the undercollar turned-back edges.

To prepare the undercollar, stitch center back seam; press open, and trim to ¼ inch (6 mm). Machine-stitch along all seam lines with matching thread. Cut interfacing of hair canvas, marking roll line with dressmaker's carbon. Join interfacing sections by overlapping seam lines and zigzagging. Trim close to stitching. Cut off all the seam allowances on interfacing and trim corners completely out of seam allowance. Pin interfacing to undercollar and machine-stitch through roll line (See Fig. 154).

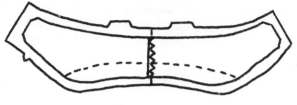

Figure 154

PAD-STITCHING UNDERCOLLAR

Keep collar in wearing position and start rows of pad-stitching by placing a row on each side of the roll line. Work small ¼ inch (6 mm) stitches on the collar stand where stiffness is desired. Stitches on the other side should be ½ inch (1.2 cm) long, but they should become smaller again in the points to help them lie flat against the body (See Fig. 155).

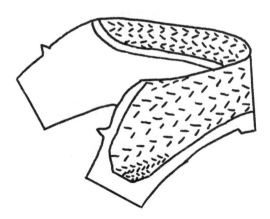

Figure 155

Trim undercollar fabric corners diagonally to the seam line, and fold in along all seam allowances. Baste close to folded edges. Press as firmly as possible, clipping curves where necessary (See Fig. 156).

Figure 156

Press while pinned to a ham as shown in Figure 157, using a lot of steam to set the shape. Press a firm crease along the roll line.

Figure 157

UPPER COLLAR

With this method, the upper collar is attached to the neck edge before the undercollar. To prepare the upper collar, stitch along the seam lines. Turn the *outer* and *side* edges along stitching, slipping the corner fold at the points away from the edge. Trim as closely as possible to eliminate bulk in the corners. Baste close to folded edges. Press as firmly as possible and trim folded edge to ⅜ inch (9mm) as shown in Figure 158.

Figure 158

Pin upper collar to neck edge of jacket, with edges even, having right side of collar and wrong side of jacket together. Ends of collar should reach to clipped corners of lapels. Baste in place, clipping jacket neck edge where necessary. Machine-stitch as basted through collar, tape, and jacket neck layers, keeping front facing and lining out of the way.

Press seam allowances toward collar. Trim seam allowances close to stitching, making sure to grade the layers.

ATTACHING UNDERCOLLAR

Pin undercollar to upper collar wrong sides together, holding collars in wearing position so that upper collar takes the outer curve. Baste, matching center back seam of undercollar and center back seam of jacket. Keep undercollar edges slightly inside of upper collar edges to prevent seam from showing when collar is worn. Hand-stitch outer folded edges using felling stitch and placing stitches about ⅛ inch (3 mm) apart (See Fig. 159).

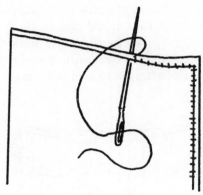

Figure 159

Slipstitch neck edge to jacket. Press collar over a ham to crease upper collar's roll line. Press all edges to obtain the sharpest edges possible.

Press under neck edge seam allowance of front facing, clipping the curve. From right side, slipstitch front facing to upper collar; make stitches very small and do not pull tightly (See Fig. 160).

Figure 160

BUTTONHOLES

Mark the placement for your buttonholes with a running basting stitch. At this point I recommend getting the jacket professionally pressed before doing the buttons and buttonholes. If there are areas that pull or wrinkle, you can still go back to the jacket to adjust. It's a good idea to hard-press the roll line with your steam iron before you send it to the cleaners so that there is no doubt as to exactly where you want that roll line. It should begin 1½ inches (3.8 cm) above the top buttonhole.

Regardless of what method you use, remember that all buttonholes should be keyholes. They should be approximately 1 inch (2.5 cm) in finished length, depending on the size of your button. Make sure you put them on the left side, ⅝ inch (1.5 cm) from the front edge.

If you have a keyhole buttonhole attachment in the correct size, you can do them by machine. Or you can do them by hand as custom tailors do. It's quite easy, but it does require some practice, so make sure you do some samples first.

Put a row of tiny machine-stitching ⅛ inch (3 mm) around the marked buttonhole, leaving an open end for the keyhole on the front edge. These tiny stitches stay the hole when it is slit and help keep everything in place (See Fig. 161).

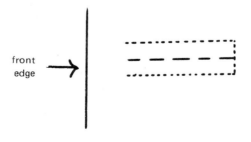

front
edge

Figure 161

Now, after the stay-stitching, slit the buttonhole, cutting out to the corners to make a triangle for the keyhole (See Fig. 162).

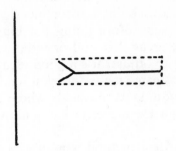

Figure 162

Cut off the triangle and round off the little corners (See Fig. 163).

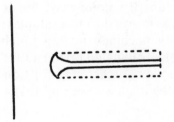

Figure 163

Measure a piece of silk twist buttonhole thread, 36 inches (91.4 cm) long. Run it through beeswax a couple of times, rubbing off the excess with your fingers. Also run another piece of twist, approximately 12 inches (30.4 cm) long, through the beeswax. String this along the opening of the buttonhole somewhat like a clothesline on two pins (See Fig. 164).

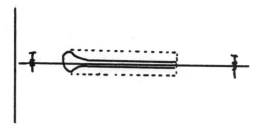

Figure 164

Move it as you work around the opening of the buttonhole, working your buttonhole stitch over it. To start your buttonhole, insert your needle just before the closed end to bury your thread (See Fig. 165).

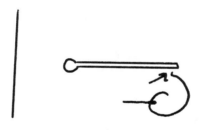

Figure 165

You want to avoid any bulky knots showing. Now, insert your needle halfway from the center of the buttonhole (the cut edge). Going over your stay-stitching, hold your needle in that position until you have made your buttonhole stitch. This is done by taking the double thread that comes out of the eye of the needle, twisting it in front of the needle, and pulling out the needle (See Fig. 166).

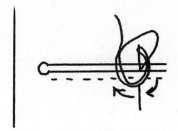

Figure 166

You will see that you have made a little "purl" with this twist. Now, pulling the thread upward, hold the purl stitch with your left thumb to keep it from sinking into the cut edge of the buttonhole (See Fig. 167).

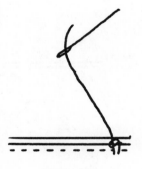

Figure 167

The secret here is that in men's tailoring, you set the purl on top of the buttonhole instead of on the edge. This gives the finished appearance of a fine line made up of purl stitches all around the buttonhole (See Fig. 168).

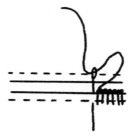

Figure 168

After you have placed the purl in the proper position, pull your thread from left to right to lock the stitch and then continue around the buttonhole (See Fig. 169).

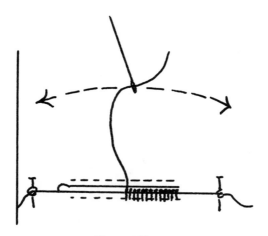

Figure 169

Your stitches should be quite close and you will be biting into the fabric, past the stay-stitching, which you use as a gauge for depth. When you have finished going completely around the buttonhole, pull the thread inside your stitches slightly to tighten the keyhole of the buttonhole. Clip the ends of the twist, make a bar-tack at the end of the buttonhole, and bury your thread. Press the completed buttonhole. The beeswax will melt and your buttonhole will look much more finished.

Spend a little time practicing on buttonholes. It will build up your confidence. You'll always find that the more your buttonholes are pressed, the more finished their appearance will be.

BUTTONS

Don't forget to sew your buttons on with a shank so that they lie smoothly when buttoned. This is easily done by holding the button in a slightly raised position while sewing it on. Then, after you have gone through the button enough times, wrap your remaining thread around the loose threads between the button and the fabric until you have formed a shank (See Fig. 170).

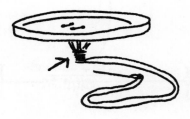

Figure 170

Some people prefer to place a toothpick or a straight pin between the fabric and button to aid them in building a shank. Then, remove the toothpick or pin and wrap the thread as described above.

For a curved-front jacket, place all buttons ⅝ inch (1.5 cm) from the front edge, except for the bottom button, which must be placed ½ inch (1.2 cm) from the edge. For all double-breasted jackets or straight-edge jackets, all buttons must be placed ⅝ inch (1.5 cm) from the front edge.

Once the buttons are on, you have completed the jacket! I hope that you are pleased and that you'll want to make another one soon. Don't forget—each jacket becomes easier to make than the last one!

CONTEMPORARY METHOD

This section uses up-to-date ideas that make tailoring a quicker process. Hand pad-stitching is replaced with fusible interfacings, and only the sleeves are lined to make the garment easy to slip on and off. Exposed seams are finished to give them a neat appearance and extra-wide front facings support the inside pocket and finish the front edge. This method is suitable only for fabrics that have body of their own, since there will be no lining for support. Polyester double knits lend themselves nicely to this method. You will have a good looking garment when you finish, but not as much controlled shaping and durability as you have when using traditional techniques. There is no reason why you can't combine the two methods by using fusible interfacings and still fully lining the jacket. I will describe the true contemporary method, and you can make adaptations as you like.

Prepare your fabric and lining as described on page 94 in this manual. Use a pattern designed to be unlined, and cut out your jacket following pattern instruction.

FRONT INTERFACING

Cut front interfacing from a fusible lightweight canvas interfacing. Mark buttonhole placement and lapel roll line on interfacing with dressmaker's carbon and tracing wheel. Carefully trim off ½ inch (1.2 cm) from the seam allowance and trim ¼ inch (6 mm) across corners to reduce bulk when turned. One eighth inch (3 mm) of interfacing will be caught in the seams. Cut a slit in the interfacing so the stitched dart can slip through before fusing.

Stitch dart in jacket front. Position interfacing on wrong side of jacket front, matching seam lines and slipping sewn dart on jacket into slit on interfacing. On fabrics that are lightweight, fuse the entire front piece or a line will show on the right side where the interfacing ends.

Fuse the interfacing to your jacket with a steam iron and wet press cloth, following manufacturer's directions. Work carefully, leaving no areas unfused. Allow the fabric to dry before removing from your ironing board (See Fig. 171).

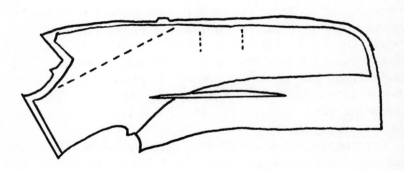

Figure 171

PADDING LAPEL POINT

Cut a triangle of interfacing to fit point of lapel between the seam allowances. Trim ¼ inch (6 mm) off corner at the point. Fuse this triangle on top of the first layer to help keep the point of your lapel turned toward the jacket (See Fig. 172).

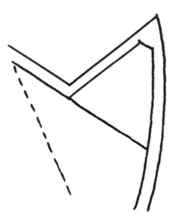

Figure 172

TAPING

TAPING ROLL LINE

Cut preshrunk ¼ inch (6 mm) twill tape for roll line as follows: Measure from 1 inch (2.5 cm) above lower end of lapel along roll line to neck seam, and then subtract ½ inch (1.2 cm) from this measurement. Cut your tape that length. Then pin tape ¼ inch (6 mm) behind roll line, starting 1 inch (2.5 cm) *above lower end of lapel and ending at the neck seam line, stretching tape to fit. Pin tape at intervals, distributing fullness evenly. Machine-stitch along each side of the twill tape, stretching tape as you stitch. This creates a natural tendency for the lapel to roll towards the outside of the jacket.*

TAPING SHOULDER

Cut pieces of twill tape ¾ inch (1.8 cm) shorter than the shoulder seam. This shortened tape reduces bulk in crossed seams. Center tape over the seam line and machine-stitch through center of tape.

FINISHING SEAMS

Since this type of jacket is unlined, some kind of seam finish is necessary to give the inside of the jacket a finished look. The best method is to encase all seams in double fold bias tape or bias made of lining fabric. On a lightweight woven fabric, seam allowances can be turned under and stitched instead of bound.

JACKET BACK

Stitch center back seam above vent; bind seam edges. Cut ¼ inch (6 mm) twill tape ¾ inches (1.8 cm) shorter than back neck seam and place on seam line. Machine-stitch through center of tape.

Tape armhole seam the same as for a traditional tailored jacket. Since the tape is stitched within the armhole seam allowance, it will not show on the inside of the unlined jacket.

HEM INTERFACING

Interfacing in the hemline adds firmness, prevents stretching, and makes a sharp hem crease.

For jacket fronts, back, and underarm pieces, cut bias strips of fusible interfacing ¼ inch (6 mm) less than the finished depth of the hem. Strips should extend from side seam to edge of interfacing on jacket, between seam allowances on underarm piece, and from side seam to start of vent on jacket back. Fuse strips above hem with one long edge exactly on hemline.

Cut interfacing for left back vent ¼ inch (6 mm) narrower than vent, extending from seam allowance at top of vent to hemline. Fuse in place over jacket behind vent. Encase vent edges in bias tape (See Fig. 173).

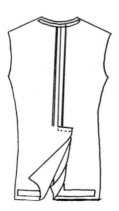

Figure 173

Cut 2 inch (5 cm) wide bias strips of interfacing for sleeves to fit along hemline between vent edges. Fuse to sleeves along hemline. Cut interfacing for sleeve vent following guidelines for back vent.

UNDERCOLLAR

Trim off seam allowances on undercollar interfacing. Fuse interfacing to undercollar sections within seam allowances. Stitch center back seam on undercollar, press open, and trim to ¼ inch (6 mm). Machine-stitch through interfacing and under-collar along roll line.

Cut a second layer of interfacing to fit from roll line to neck seam line. To cut, place center back seam line along bias fold of interfacing fabric to eliminate center back seam on this layer. Fuse second layer to undercollar over trimmed and pressed center back collar seam (See Fig. 174).

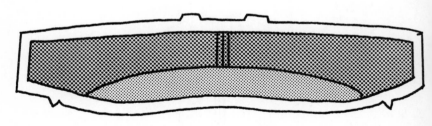

Figure 174

Fold undercollar along roll line, interfacing side out. Pin around a ham and steam press to shape. Allow collar to dry before removing from ham (See Fig. 175).

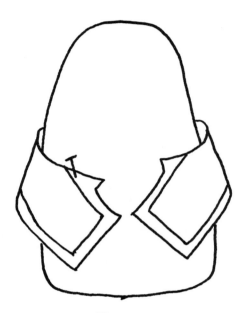

Figure 175

Clip curve on neck edge of jacket back, being careful not to clip tape. Pin undercollar to jacket neck edge, right sides together, matching center back and notches. Stitch, with collar side up, from one collar seam allowance to the other. Stitching must begin and end exactly at seam allowance to insure a smooth corner when turned. Trim seam allowances; clip curves. Press the neck seam allowance open from shoulder seam to end of stitching. Press back neck seam allowance toward collar.

SHOULDER PADS AND SLEEVES

The shoulder pad fills out the hollow in a man's chest just beneath his shoulder and gives the shoulder a smooth line. Cover shoulder pads in an unlined jacket with your lining fabric so they will have a finished look on the inside of your jacket.

Sew sleeves into your jacket following your pattern guide. Trim seam allowance to ¼ inch (6 mm) below the notches. Press seam open above the notches, then trim seam allowances to ⅜ inch (9 mm).

Try on jacket to pin shoulder pads in place. One third of the pad goes in front, two thirds in back. Pad should extend ⅜ inch (9 mm) beyond armhole seam and even with trimmed seam allowance.

From the outside of the jacket, baste pad in place along shoulder seam and ½ inch (1.2 cm) from armhole seam. Basting should go through all thicknesses of jacket and pad.

Take off jacket and turn it inside out to anchor pad permanently. Turn back the armhole edge of the shoulder pad and slipstitch to jacket at the sleeve seam. Tack the free edge of the pad to the shoulder seam allowance.

SLEEVE HEAD

The sleeve head gives the top of the sleeve cap a smooth line and improves the hang of the sleeve. Follow the directions on page 130 of this manual.

FACING AND UPPER COLLAR

PREPARING FACING AND UPPER COLLAR

The inside welt pocket is made entirely on the extra-wide jacket front facing using lining fabric for the pocket. Follow the directions on page 131 for complete instructions.

Bind shoulder and inner edges of front facing with bias seam binding. Machine-stitch on neck seam line of facing as a guide for turning under seam allowance.

Machine-stitch on seam lines of upper collar to prevent fabric from stretching and to serve as a guide for turning under back neck seam allowance.

Clip curved neck edge of facing to stitching. Right sides together, pin upper collar to neck edge of front facings, matching seam lines and notches. Stitch from medium dot on facing to end of facing. Clip facing to medium dot at end of collar and to small dot at shoulder seam. Press seam allowance open between clips. Trim seams; clip curves. Turn under back neck edge of collar along machine-stiching, clipping curves. Trim to ¼ inch (6 mm).

ATTACHING FACING AND UPPER COLLAR

Right sides together, pin facing and upper collar to jacket and undercollar, matching notches, center back and dots. Stitch facing and upper collar to jacket and undercollar, beginning at center back of collar and working towards lower edge of facing. Stitch along outer edge of collar to medium dot at neckline *seam, eliminating collar seam allowances; secure stitches. Begin stitching again at medium dot, eliminating facing seam allowances. Stitch to point of lapel, taking two stitches across point to facilitate turning. Stitch to end of facing at lower edge of jacket. Repeat for other side, beginning at center back of collar (See Fig. 176).*

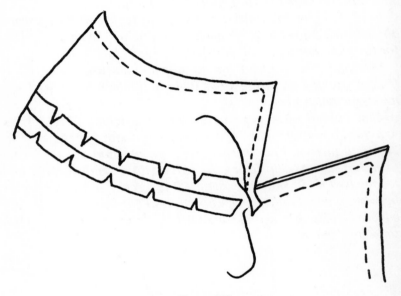

Figure 176

Grade seam. Trim free collar and facing neck seam allowances to ¼ inch (6 mm), trimming diagonally at medium dot. Turn upper collar facing edge so seam is on the inside from lower edge of jacket to lower end of lapel and on the outside along lapel and collar edges. Rolling the seam in this manner prevents it from showing when pressed in place.

Smooth facing over shoulder pad, then slipstitch facing to shoulder seam of the jacket. Sew facing to armhole seam allowances with long hand stitches in matching thread. Raw edges will be covered by the sleeve lining.

Pin pressed neck edge of upper collar over back neck seam, matching centers. Slipstitch in place.

FINISHING HEMS AND VENTS

Enclose raw edges of hem in bias seam binding. Turn up hem and catch-stitch in place, having stitches between binding and jacket. Turn in left back vent along fold line. Finish vent according to your pattern directions.

SLEEVE LININGS

Stitch seams in sleeve lining from armhole to lower edge, omitting vent. Press seams open. Ease-stitch top of sleeve lining. Turn jacket sleeve and lining sleeve wrong sides out. Match the pressed-open underarm seams, keeping armhole edges even. With long running stitches, sew one seam allowance of the lining to matching seam allowance of the sleeve, starting and ending about 4 inches (10.2 cm) from top and bottom of the sleeve.

Slip your hand inside the sleeve lining from the armhole. Grasp the lower edge of the jacket sleeve and the lining and pull them both through the lining. The lining should be right side out over the jacket sleeve.

Pin the lining to the armhole, matching notches, and underarm and shoulder seams. Pull up ease-stitching and distribute ease, fitting lining over the sleeve. Sew lining over sleeve seam with small firm hemming stitches. Where lining covers shoulder pad, slipstitch lining to pad ⅜ inch (9 mm) from pad edge.

Baste lining to sleeve about 4 inches (10.2 cm) above hem. Turn under lining hem allowance, press, and baste. Hem lining over sleeve hem with small stitches, allowing a pleat to form in lining for ease.

MEN'S PANTS

Making pants has become a very popular area of home sewing. There are a large variety of patterns to choose from, and the accompanying work sheets are a satisfactory guide for good results. However, you will want to custom-tailor the pants you sew, and I will give you tips on how to make them special.

From my own personal experience and from students' comments, I find that the first pair of pants can be difficult. However, like everything else, once you have learned a few special techniques and get the fitting problems solved, you'll be able to tailor men's pants with ease.

The suggestions in this section of the book are compatible with any purchased pattern. Your pattern guide will be your best source of information for various pockets and for inserting a fly zipper. My comments will be *additional* aids to help you finish pants professionally.

FITTING

The most important aspect of making pants is the fit. If you understand the principles that are involved in making pants that fit well, it will help you to attain the overall results you want. *Beware* of cutting out a woven fabric from a knits-only pattern. Knits-only patterns are made with the elasticity of the fabric incorporated into the cut, and they fit the body more snugly. However, you can make knit pants from patterns calling for regular fabrics.

The best way to begin is to make a muslin mock-up. Or: Take a good-fitting pair of pants and carefully measure the crotch seams. If the best-fitting pants' measurements differ greatly from those of the pattern you have selected, you will need to alter the pattern accordingly before cutting and sewing. Remember that boys tend to wear their pants lower on the hip than mature men. You should buy the pattern according to waist size—unless hips are unusually large. If so, buy the hip measurement and adjust the waistline.

After you have made up the basic muslin, check the depth of the crotch and the fit of the hips and waist. Then make any necessary adjustments on your pattern.

The key to a good fit is actually the crotch seam. This controls the fit in both front and back for comfort. Some men may need more in the back for a rounded seat. You would then add more length in the back. If you have a round tummy to contend with, then add more length in front (See Fig. 177).

As you can see, in men's tailoring, alterations are made on a common sense basis. There is very little splitting, folding, or slashing of patterns. Cut larger for more cloth to cover an area, or reduce the amount of cloth to compensate for a smaller area.

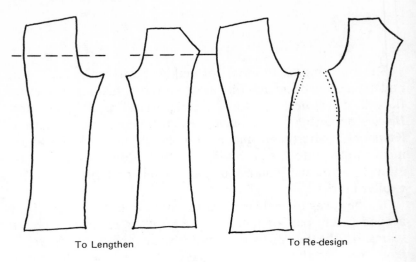

To Lengthen   To Re-design

Figure 177

CUTTING

After alterations have been made, transfer them to your pattern. Use your own favorite cutting and marking techniques.

Most tailors cut the left front crotch side slightly larger than the right side—especially on the popular slim-fitting pants. Add ¾ inch (1.8 cm) to the left side of your pattern and this will give you the extra room needed for comfort in this area (See Fig. 178).

Also, cut a let-out seam (large seam allowance) in the center back if the pattern has not already allowed for it (See Fig. 179). Make sure that the additional fabric allowance starts wider at the waist and gradually tapers down to nothing at the lower portion of the seat. Stitch on the *original* seam line.

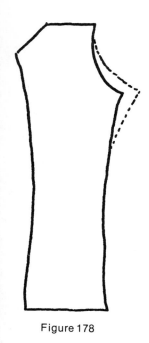

Figure 178

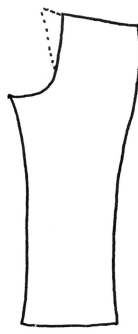

Figure 179

Use professional pocket material or a firmly woven cotton for your pockets. Check the finished depth and check to make sure it's ample. Often patterns have skimpy pockets. To make them larger, simply cut pockets deeper. Back pockets should be approximately 6 inches (15.2 cm) in depth. Front pockets will vary more according to style.

Also, check your pattern to make sure the back welt pockets are placed properly on the back of the pants, and are not set too high. A standard professional tailoring rule is that the back welt pocket should be placed at the tip of the back dart. If you change their placement, make sure the pocket extensions into the waistband are cut longer also. And be sure to move the facings so they will correspond to the new length (See Fig. 180).

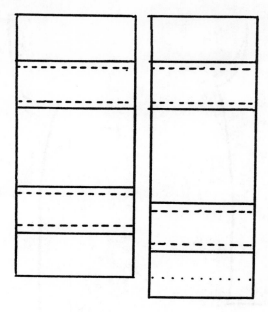

Figure 180

SEWING PREPARATION

Mark all construction marks carefully after cutting. Do not omit any markings, as accuracy is essential when professionally tailoring a pair of pants.

Attaching crotch liners will prolong the pants' wear and make them more comfortable. The liners are cut from the pocketing material. Cut two on the bias, folded in half and placed at the raw edges of the front crotch. Line up even to the front crotch and leg seams and machine-stitch ½ inch (1.2 cm) from the raw edges (See Fig. 181).

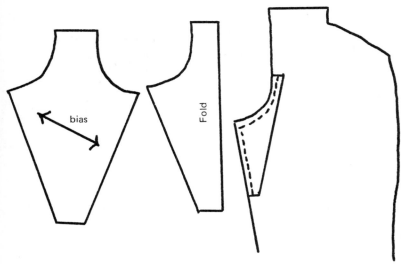

Figure 181

For best results, press the creases of the pants in before you begin to do any sewing. Simply bring the side seam edges together and press. Be sure to use a press cloth if your fabric tends to shine. Do all four sections. When you press the backs, it is a good idea to stretch the crotch area up toward the back seam. This slight shaping helps to give that desired professional look (See Fig. 182).

Sew in back darts now, if not already done.

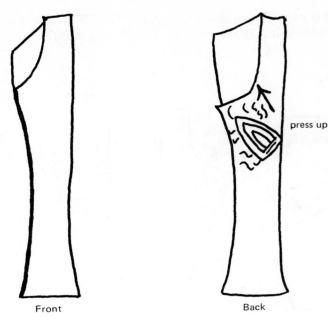

press up

Front   Back

Figure 182

BACK POCKETS

It is easiest to construct the back welt pockets now before other pieces are attached. Pattern designs differ, and it is best at this point to follow the directions of your commercial pattern.

The top parts of the pocket will extend into the waistband area. Check to make sure they will (See Fig. 183).

Here is *one* method for inserting the single welt pocket, which is the most common style for the back pants' pocket. It is made of one welt, one pocket piece, and a facing that ends off behind the welt.

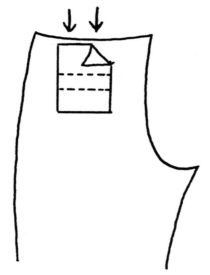

Figure 183

After stitching dart, prepare the pieces for the back pockets, back pocket facings, and welts. The welt can be interfaced to its fold or fused in half lengthwise with a fusible web. Baste the welt to the outside of pants' back along lower pocket marking as shown in Fig. 184. Stitch along stitching line, securing the thread ends.

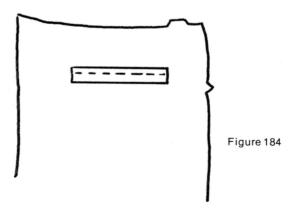

Figure 184

To prepare the facing, press under ¼ inch (6 mm) on one long edge as shown in Fig. 185.

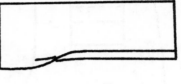

Figure 185

Facing can be simply fused in place or it can be basted in place before machine-stitching close to the folded edge (See Fig. 186).

Press ¼ inch (6 mm) on the long edges of the pocket to the right side, and machine-stitch close to the fold (See Fig. 187).

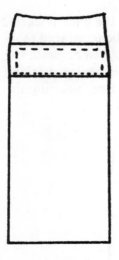

Figure 186

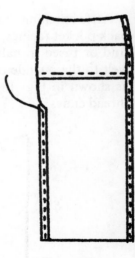

Figure 187

Pin unfaced end of pocket face down over the welt. Baste the pocket along pocket lines, accurately matching the markings. Stitch along the two stitching lines, securing thread ends. Do not stitch across the ends of pocket lines. Slash pocket and pants between the stitching to about ½ inch (1.2 cm) from ends. Clip diagonally to the outer corners, being careful not to cut into welt (See Fig. 188).

Figure 188

Bring the pocket, clipped V-shaped corners, and ends of the welt through the slash to the inside of the pants. Machine-stitch clipped corners and ends of welts together, as illustrated in Fig. 189.

Fold pocket along foldline with cut edge extending to waistline and markings matched. Pin sides of pocket together. Machine-stitch ⅜ inch (9 mm) from the folded edges along the

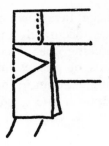

Figure 189

seam line, stitching below upper pocket lines and catching in the V-shaped corners. Stitch again close to the folded edges (See Fig. 190). This will encase the cut edges and give a neat appearance to the inside of the pants.

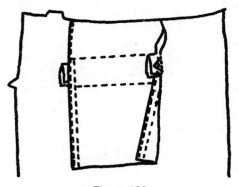

Figure 190

To finish the upper side of the pocket, fold down the waistline edge and pin pocket and slashed edges together, as shown in Figure 191. Baste securely through the thicknesses. Machine-stitch to ends of pocket opening, being sure to secure the thread ends.

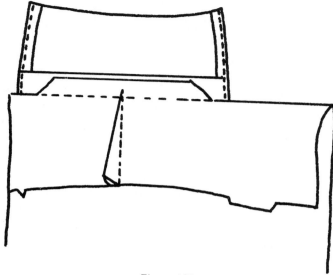

Figure 191

Baste the upper cut edge of the pocket to pants' waistline. You may choose to stitch around the pocket opening close to the ends and upper edge in order to stabilize the opening. Bartacks are often placed vertically at each end to strengthen the pocket opening (See Fig. 192).

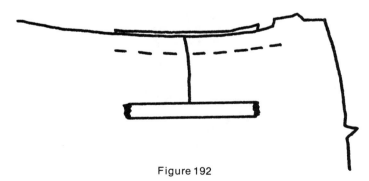

Figure 192

FRONT FLY ZIPPER

This method of inserting a front fly zipper results in a truly hand-tailored finish. The fly shield extension is added for extra security; and the edges of the fly shield are clean-finished, a technique found in ready-to-wear garments.

Before you begin, mark the curve for topstitching on the *left* front. Place the two front pieces together and stitch the front crotch seam, starting at the dot marked on your pattern and ending 1-1½ inches (2.5-3.8 cm) from the edge of inside leg (See Fig. 193). Then, with right sides together, pin the left fly facing to the left front edge, matching markings. Stitch from the marking at the bottom of the fly facing to the waist (See Fig. 193). Trim and grade seam allowances. Open out facing and press seam allowances toward the facing.

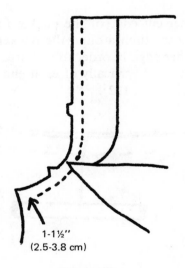

1-1½"
(2.5-3.8 cm)

Figure 193

Next, position the closed zipper face down on the right side
of the facing. The right edge of the zipper tape should lie along
the facing seam and the bottom stop of the zipper should be ¾
inch (1.8 cm) from the raw edge of the facing. The top of the
zipper may extend beyond the upper edge of the facing. Pin the
zipper in place, with the bottom of the right zipper tape up on
itself even with the bottom stop, so it will not be caught in the
outer topstitching later. Baste the right edge of the tape to the
facing from bottom to top. On the left tape, stitch close to coil,
using your zipper foot and regular stitch length. Stitch again,
close to the edge of tape (See Fig. 194). Turn the facing to inside
on seamline and press in position.

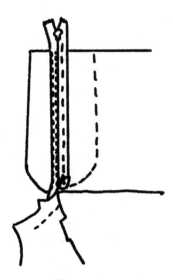

Figure 194

On the outside of your garment, pin front to fly facing and topstitch from the bottom to the top along your previously basted marking, being careful not to catch in the right side of the zipper tape (See Fig. 195). Pull threads to the wrong side and tie. Remove basting.

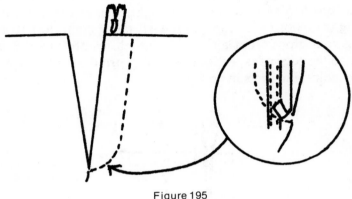

Figure 195

Now, work begins on the *right* fly shield and extension. The extension is found on expensive ready-made pants, and it gives additional support to the waist fasteners. Make the fly shield extension following the pattern in Figure 196 if one is not included in your pattern. Cut two pieces from pants' fabric (or one from lining and one from pants' fabric, if your fabric is bulky); then stitch these pieces together in a ¼ inch (6 mm) seam, leaving the short straight edge open for turning. Trim seam, turn, and press. Make a machine-worked buttonhole at the marking.

Position extension (as shown by dotted lines in Fig. 197) between right sides of fly shield and fly shield lining. Stitch along unnotched curved edge of fly shield, catching open end of extension in stitching. Trim, grade, and clip seam allowances; turn and press.

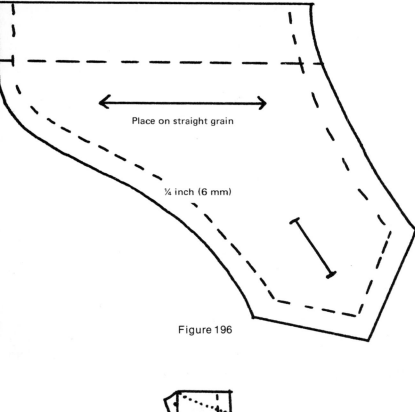

Place on straight grain

¼ inch (6 mm)

Figure 196

Figure 197

To finish raw edge of fly shield, trim ⅜ inch (9 mm) from pants' fabric on notched edge. Fold lining over raw edge of pants' fabric and stitch close to the fold (See Fig. 198).

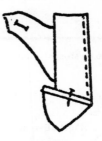

Figure 198

On pants *right* front, press under ¼ inch (6 mm) on notched edge; pin the fold to the free zipper tape, close to the coil. To position the fly *shield,* work from the wrong side and match pin temporarily as in Figure 199. Turn the unit back to the right side and repin right front and zipper tape to the long straight edge of the fly shield. Open your zipper; using the zipper foot, stitch through all thicknesses (front, zipper tape, and fly shield) from top to bottom close to the zipper coil (See Fig. 200).

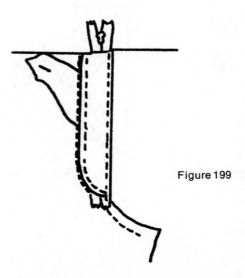

Figure 199

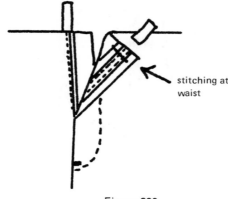

stitching at
waist

Figure 200

Pull thread ends to the wrong side and tie.

While the zipper is still *open,* stitch across the zipper tapes at waistline and cut off excess zipper (See Fig. 200). *Note:* This must be done with the zipper open, so that the slider is not cut off!

Work a bar-tack by hand or machine at the bottom of the fly, catching in the fly shield.

FRONT POCKETS

Insert the ranch pockets or side pockets on the front section of the pants, according to your pattern. The inside raw edges will differ in finishing, depending upon the design of the pocket. Some pockets will be constructed so that you can finish them off as you did the back pockets. Other pockets can only be stitched together on the inside of the pants, and the edges will have to be zigzagged for a finished look (See Fig. 201).

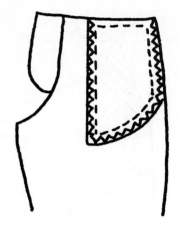

Figure 201

The extra time and effort you spend in constructing nicely finished pants *inside* will pay off in far better service and longer life than any ready-to-wear slacks can give.

If you did not join the side leg seams when you inserted the side pockets, do it now. Then, join the *inside* seams of the legs. The center back seam is left open for the time being.

WAISTBAND

The waistband of men's pants is unlike most women's pants. For menswear, a stiffener is used and the waistband is cut in two pieces, one left and one right. For ease in altering, the center back seam is finished after the two waistband sections have been applied. A "V" in the center back waistband seam provides flexibility. I will describe two waistband methods: One uses a commercial product with the stiffener attached to a facing, and the other uses a separate stiffener and a facing cut on the bias from lining fabric.

METHOD I: Waistband with commercial facing

From the pants' fabric, cut the waistband 1¼ inch (3.2 cm) wider than the commercial facing. Use your pattern piece to determine the length of each waistband piece and to mark the notches.

Cut the commercial facing the same length as your waistband strips. Study Figure 202 to familiarize yourself with the construction of the commercial product.

Figure 202

With right sides together, stitch fabric waistband to each half of the pants, matching notches and stitching *exactly* at ⅝ inch (1.5 cm). Grade and press the seam toward the waistband.

Press under ½ inch (1.2 cm) on the top edge of the lining. Sandwich the free edge of the waistband between the stiffener and the lining, placing the raw edge of the waistband along the inner edge of the reinforcement or stiffener. Topstitch along the fold through all thicknesses of stiffener-lining (See Fig. 203).

Finish the front of each section of waistband by turning right sides together and stitching ⅝ inch (1.5 cm) from the front raw edge. Grade seam, turn, and press.

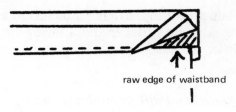

raw edge of waistband

Figure 203

With waistband lining extended up and out of the way, sew the back crotch seam, beginning ⅜ inch (9 mm) below the edge of the stiffener and tapering to meet front crotch seam below the fly front. The waistband lining is not seamed in this stitching.

Press the back crotch seam open, including the unstitched waistband lining. Fold one side of the waistband out of the way. On the remaining section, open out seam allowances and fold the waistband so the right sides are together. Stitch in pressed crease; do not trim seam (See Fig. 204). Turn the waistband right side out and entire facing to the wrong side. Repeat for the other side. Press.

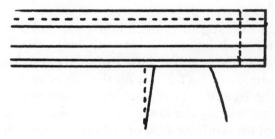

Figure 204

You will have to determine where you want to put the hooks and eyes *now* because they often have to be inserted before the waistband is closed up. If you check ready-made pants, you will notice there are many ways to finish them. *Your* finishing will depend upon your pattern and upon what you prefer. If you are finishing off the waistband with buttons, be sure that some of the facing is trimmed away in that area so that you will not have bulky buttonholes.

To finish waistband, "stitch in the ditch" from the right side of the garment, lifting the lining pleat out of the way on the wrong side and stitching only through under pleat of stiffener (See Fig. 205).

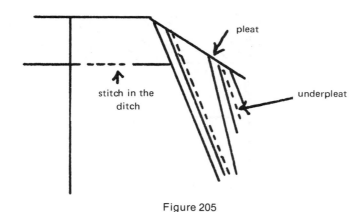

Figure 205

METHOD II: Waistband with separate facing and stiffener

The stiffener should be purchased in the width you wish the finished waistband to be.

From the pants' fabric, cut the waistband 1½ inch (3.8 cm) wider than the stiffener. Use the pattern piece to determine the length and to mark the notches.

From the lining fabric, cut a bias facing 2½ inch (5.7 cm) wider than the stiffener and the length of your waistband. Press under 1 inch (2.5 cm) on one long edge of each bias strip. Cut stiffener the length of each half of the waistband, minus ⅝ inch (1.5 cm). Make sure that the stiffener does not extend into the front seam allowance.

With right sides together, stitch fabric waistband to each half of pants, matching notches and stitching exactly at ⅝ inch (1.5 cm). Position stiffener on waistband seam allowances. Topstitch as shown in Figure 206. Grade seam and press waistband up.

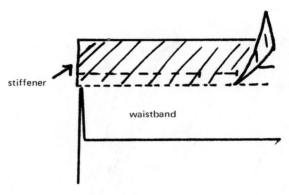

stiffener

waistband

Figure 206

To attach the facing, place raw edge of facing to raw edge at top of waistband, right sides together. Stitch exactly ⅝ inch (1.5 cm) from raw edge. Turn facing to wrong side. There will be ¼ inch (6 mm) between facing and top of waistband. Press (See Fig. 207).

Finish front edges and back seam as described in Method I. Attach fasteners and then turn waistband to wrong side and stitch in the ditch *through* lining.

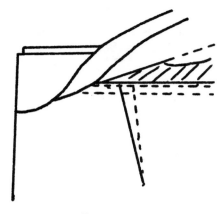

Figure 207

With both methods, any areas of the front portions of the waistband facing that come too close to the zipper area will have to be turned under diagonally and slipstitched in place.

WAISTBAND CARRIERS

The belt loops or carriers are stitched on *last.* If your pattern has one of the new wider waistbands, your carriers must be wider and longer to accommodate the new wide belts. Again, there are many methods of installing belt loops. The method I will describe is the one I have found to be the easiest.

Fold a strip of fabric into thirds. Top stitch each folded side. Cut for desired length. With knits, it is a good idea to insert a small strip of light interfacing to add stability. The cut side will always be placed underneath.

To attach, place the *right side* of the carriers against the right side of the pants, stitching near the raw edge to the top of the pants, through all thicknesses (See Fig. 208).

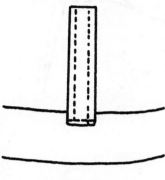

Figure 208

Then turn the carrier down, fold under the raw edge, and topstitch near the folded edge, through all thicknesses, to anchor the bottom of each carrier (See Fig. 209).

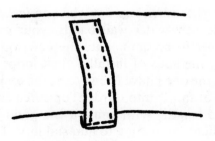

Figure 209

HEMS

Hems on the pants' legs can be finished off by pinking the raw edge, running a machine-stitch ¼ inch (6 mm) from the raw edge, and invisibly catch-stitching the hem to the pants. If you have flared bottoms, it's a good idea to take a small dart in the back hemline to aid the drape in the back and to shape (See Fig. 210).

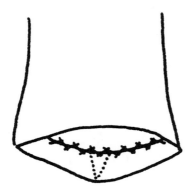

Figure 210

With the creases already established, you merely have to press the pants. For a really finished look, be sure you end off with *sharp* creases.

Once you have finished your first pair of pants, you will find future pairs considerably easier and faster to make.

Index